contents

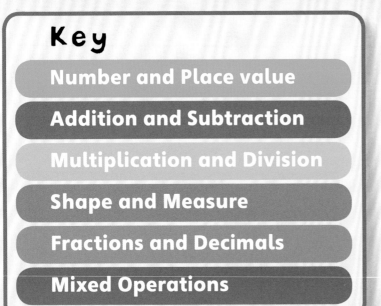

Key

- Number and Place value
- Addition and Subtraction
- Multiplication and Division
- Shape and Measure
- Fractions and Decimals
- Mixed Operations

How to use this book

Read the instructions carefully before each set of questions.

The first page of each section will have a title telling you what the next few pages are about.

Some pages will show you an example or model.

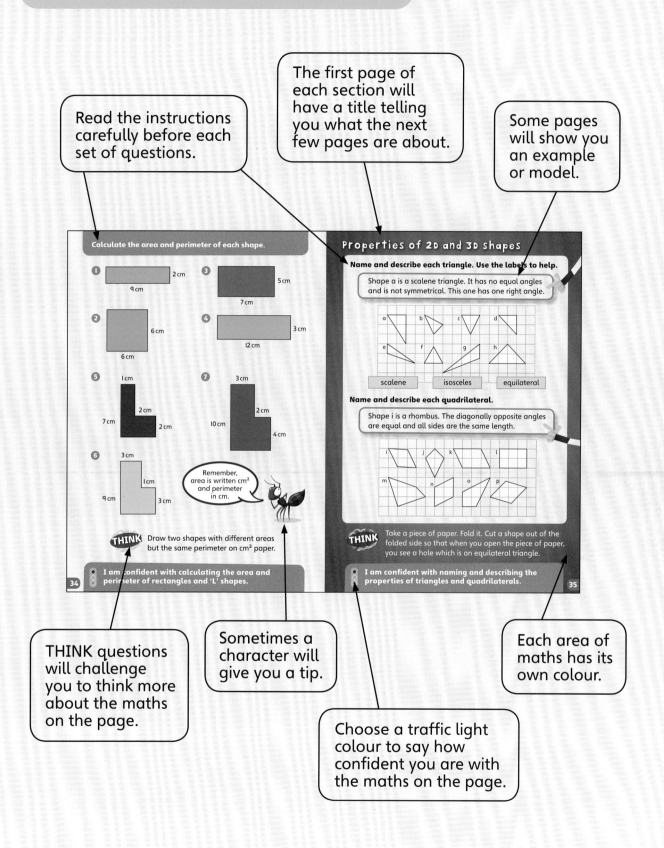

Calculate the area and perimeter of each shape.

1. 2 cm, 9 cm
2. 6 cm, 6 cm
3. 5 cm, 7 cm
4. 3 cm, 12 cm
5. 1 cm, 2 cm, 7 cm, 2 cm
6. 3 cm, 1 cm, 9 cm, 3 cm
7. 3 cm, 2 cm, 10 cm, 4 cm

Remember, area is written cm² and perimeter in cm.

THINK Draw two shapes with different areas but the same perimeter on cm² paper.

I am confident with calculating the area and perimeter of rectangles and 'L' shapes.

34

Properties of 2D and 3D shapes

Name and describe each triangle. Use the labels to help.

Shape a is a scalene triangle. It has no equal angles and is not symmetrical. This one has one right angle.

a b c d
e f g h

scalene   isosceles   equilateral

Name and describe each quadrilateral.

Shape i is a rhombus. The diagonally opposite angles are equal and all sides are the same length.

i j k l
m n o p

THINK Take a piece of paper. Fold it. Cut a shape out of the folded side so that when you open the piece of paper, you see a hole which is an equilateral triangle.

I am confident with naming and describing the properties of triangles and quadrilaterals.

35

THINK questions will challenge you to think more about the maths on the page.

Sometimes a character will give you a tip.

Choose a traffic light colour to say how confident you are with the maths on the page.

Each area of maths has its own colour.

3

4-digit numbers

Write these numbers out in digits.

1. seven thousand, two hundred and ninety-three

2. eight thousand, nine hundred and forty-seven

3. six thousand, five hundred and two

4. two thousand and sixty-seven

5. three thousand, four hundred and eighty

Write < or > signs between each pair of numbers.

6. 7521   3860

7. 8353   3699

8. 9442   9852

9. 4725   4572

10. 8244   9241

11. 3026   3211

Write a number that comes between each pair of numbers.

12. 2010   4800

13. 1600   2000

14. 5650   6820

15. 4356   5073

 **THINK** Write two numbers less than 3000 using the digits 2, 4, 0 and 5. These digits have to be in each number once and the numbers must be different, but both should have five 10s.

● I am confident with reading, writing and ordering
○
○ 4-digit numbers.

Write these numbers in figures.

1. seven thousand and three
2. four thousand and forty-four
3. three thousand, six hundred and fifty-eight
4. five thousand and sixty
5. six thousand, five hundred and two

Write < or > signs between each pair of numbers.

6. 3262   1284
7. 4323   4723
8. 2010   1999

9. 2479   2749
10. 3524   3546
11. 6676   6667

Write a number that comes between each pair of numbers.

12. 2050   2500
13. 3678   4252
14. 8675   9200

15. 1999   2020
16. 4980   5126
17. 5005   5305

 **THINK** Use the digits 2, 4, 6 and 7 to write six 4-digit numbers and write them in order from smallest to largest.

I am confident with reading, writing and ordering 4-digit numbers.

5

Write these numbers out in digits.

1. two thousand, eight hundred and two

2. five thousand and fifty-five

3. nine thousand and nine

4. seven thousand, six hundred and sixteen

5. eight thousand and eleven

Write these sets of numbers in order, from smallest to largest.

6. 2854   3045   2012

7. 5015   5510   5105

8. 4786   4876   4687

Write two numbers in between each pair of numbers.

9. 1645   1924

10. 5445   5545

11. 2884   2999

12. 6950   7000

13. 9200   9002

14. 3856   3811

 **THINK** Use only the digits 1 and 5 to make this number sentence true:

☐☐☐☐ < ☐☐☐☐ < ☐☐☐☐

 **I am confident with reading, writing and ordering 4-digit numbers.**

Fill in the missing numbers for these sections of grid.

1

	2200	

100	200	300	400
1100	1200	1300	1400
2100	2200	2300	2400
3100	3200	3300	
4100	4200		

2

	3300	

3

	6800	

4

	5600	

Work out the answers to these calculations.

5 $4269 + 100 = \square$

   $4269 + 1000 = \square$

6 $5099 + 100 = \square$

   $5099 + 1000 = \square$

7 $4269 - 100 = \square$

   $4269 - 1000 = \square$

8 $5099 - 100 = \square$

   $5099 - 1000 = \square$

 If you start at 4968 and count back in steps of 100, would you ever get to 4234? Explain why or why not.

● I am confident with the place value of
○ 4-digit numbers.

5-digit numbers

Write the numbers in each set in words.

① 20 000

② 60 000

   23 000

   67 000

   23 100

   67 500

> Remember to say how many thousands each number has.

Write < or > signs between each pair of numbers.

③ 43 000   52 000

⑤ 34 000   38 000

④ 76 000   24 000

⑥ 25 200   25 600

Write a number that comes between each pair.

⑦ 20 000 and 40 000

⑨ 70 000 and 80 000

⑧ 40 000 and 60 000

⑩ 80 000 and 90 000

THINK What is the smallest 5-digit number?
What is the largest 5-digit number?

● I am confident with reading, writing and comparing
5-digit numbers.

Write these numbers in figures.

1. twenty-eight thousand, five hundred

2. thirty-four thousand, three hundred and fifty

3. sixty-eight thousand, seven hundred and twenty-five

4. forty thousand, four hundred and fifty-two

5. thirteen thousand, nine hundred and eighty-six

Write < or > signs between each pair of numbers.

6. 65 320   39 463

7. 82 700   55 460

8. 70 999   80 010

9. 73 000   73 200

10. 18 630   13 810

11. 33 009   33 900

Write a number that comes between each pair.

12. 10 000 and 11 000

13. 34 280 and 32 540

14. 15 469 and 15 800

15. 73 758 and 73 911

16. 66 202 and 65 000

17. 80 500 and 80 100

THINK   2   7   4   5   3

Using these digits, write two numbers between 40 000 and 50 000.

○ I am confident with reading, writing and comparing
○ 5-digit numbers.
○

9

Negative numbers

Write these temperatures in order, from the coldest to the hottest.

① −2, 4, 3　　④ 2, 5, −3　　⑦ −3, 8, 6

② −7, 2, 7　　⑤ 4, −1, 12　　⑧ −1, 1, 0

③ −5, 1, 0　　⑥ −9, 10, 3　　⑨ −6, 5, −8

Solve these problems.

⑩ It is −4 °C. The sun comes out and the temperature rises by 6 degrees. What is the temperature now?

Use the thermometer to count on.

⑪ It is −1 °C. The sun comes out and the temperature rises by 9 degrees. What is the temperature now?

⑫ It is −8 °C. The sun comes out and the temperature rises by 10 degrees. What is the temperature now?

⑬ It is −10°C. The sun comes out and the temperature rises by 20 degrees. What is the temperature now?

°C
15
14
13
12
11
10
9
8
7
6
5
4
3
2
1
0
−1
−2
−3
−4
−5
−6
−7
−8
−9
−10

THINK Write two temperatures found on the thermometer that have a difference of 8 degrees. One should be positive and the other negative.

 **I am confident with ordering and comparing negative numbers.**

Write these temperatures in order, from the coldest to the hottest.

1. −16, 12, −4, 1, 5

2. −1, 1, −4, 0, 6

3. −12, 4, −6, 1, 3

4. 8, 14, −14, −7, 2

5. 4, −1, 9, −10, 7

6. −9, −10, 3, 2, 8

7. −3, 4, 6, 2, −9

8. 7, 9, −1, 2, −3

9. −3, −4, −7, −1, −2

10. −2, −9, 11, −12, 15

°C

Solve these problems.

11. What is the difference between −4 °C and 14 °C?

12. What is the difference between −10 °C and −2 °C?

13. What is the difference between −13 °C and 3 °C?

14. The temperature was −5 °C. It falls by 6 degrees. What is the temperature now?

15. The temperature was −11 °C. It rises by 2 degrees. What is the temperature now?

16. The temperature is −20 °C. By how much must it rise to reach −5 °C?

 **THINK** Write two temperatures that are below zero with a difference of 7 degrees. Which is the colder temperature?

I am confident with ordering negative numbers and finding the difference between a positive and negative number.

Compare the bank balances of:

Aiza	Susan	Michael	Ahmed	Christophe
£125	−£65	−£120	£70	−£82

1. How much greater is £70 than −£82?

2. How much greater is £125 than −£65?

3. How much less is −£82 than −£65?

4. How much less is −£120 than −£82?

Solve these problems.

5. Michael is paid £200. How much is in his bank account now?

6. £20 goes out of Susan's account. What is her bank balance now?

7. Christophe is paid £50. How much is in his bank account now?

8. £80 goes out of Ahmed's account. What is his bank balance now?

THINK You have £75. £5 is coming out of your account every day for seven days due to a problem with the bank. How much money have you got left at the end of the week?

I am confident with comparing positive and negative numbers and adding to and subtracting from both.

12

understanding decimals

Write < or > between each pair of decimal numbers.

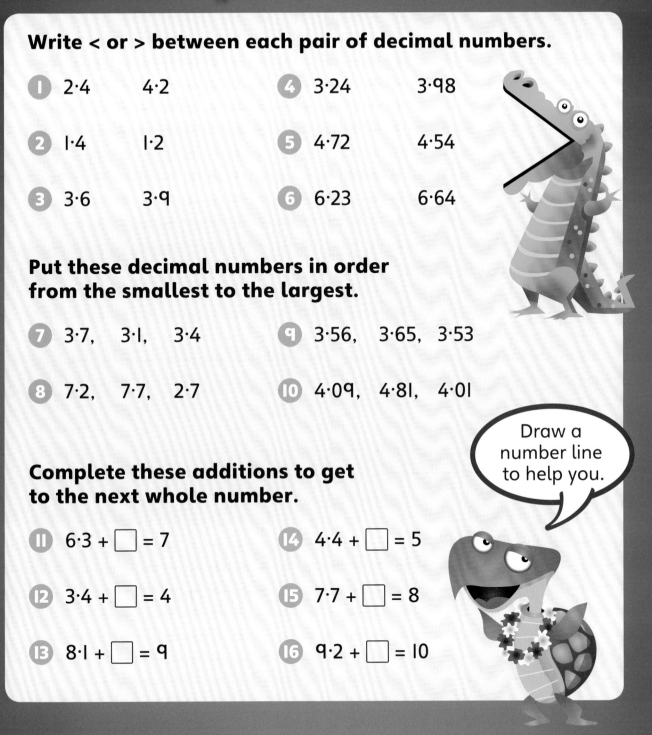

① 2·4   4·2

② 1·4   1·2

③ 3·6   3·9

④ 3·24   3·98

⑤ 4·72   4·54

⑥ 6·23   6·64

Put these decimal numbers in order
from the smallest to the largest.

⑦ 3·7,   3·1,   3·4

⑧ 7·2,   7·7,   2·7

⑨ 3·56,   3·65,   3·53

⑩ 4·09,   4·81,   4·01

Complete these additions to get
to the next whole number.

> Draw a number line to help you.

⑪ 6·3 + ☐ = 7

⑫ 3·4 + ☐ = 4

⑬ 8·1 + ☐ = 9

⑭ 4·4 + ☐ = 5

⑮ 7·7 + ☐ = 8

⑯ 9·2 + ☐ = 10

THINK   Write two numbers which have nine
1-place decimal numbers between
them. Can you easily repeat this?

I am confident with ordering decimals and adding
to them to reach the next whole number.

Put these numbers in order from the smallest to the largest.

1 3·4   3·9   3·5

2 6   6·2   2·2

3 1·4   0·4   0·7

4 3·64   6·43   4·36

5 7·25   7·02   7·89

6 5·61   6·01   5·99

7 8·84   9·01   8·49

8 2·77   2·73   2·80

Write the numbers being described as decimals.

9   seven and three-tenths and four-hundredths

10 four and six-tenths

11 nine and seven-tenths and eight-hundredths

THINK Write three decimal numbers between 2 and 3 where none of them have any tenths. Write them in order, from smallest to largest.

I am confident with writing and ordering decimals.

14

Write what the tag numbers are.

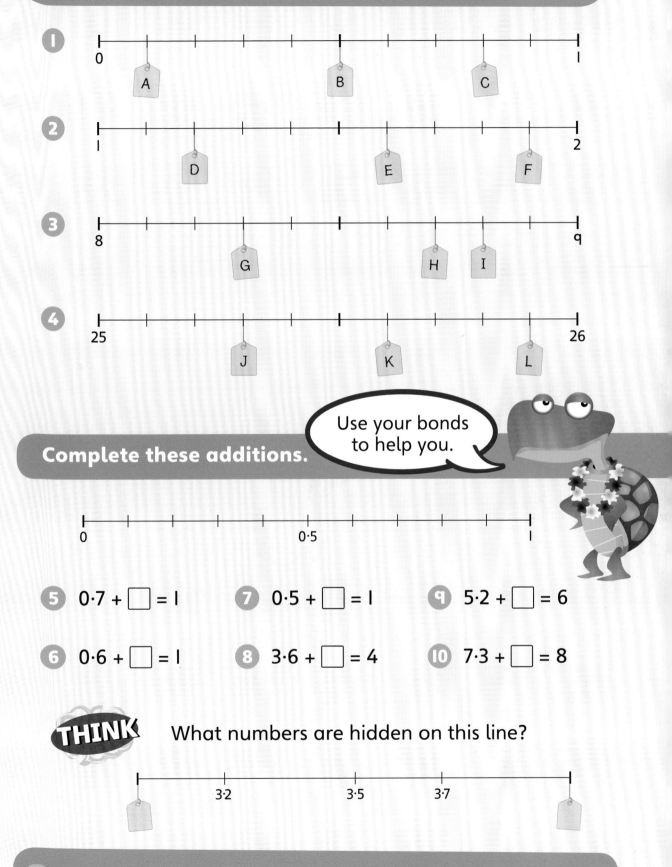

1
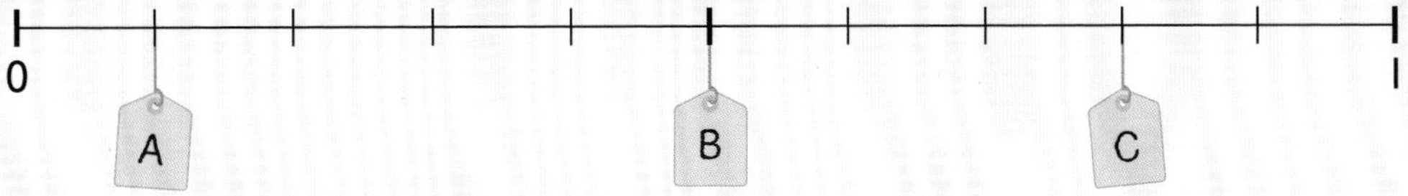
0
1
A
B
C

2
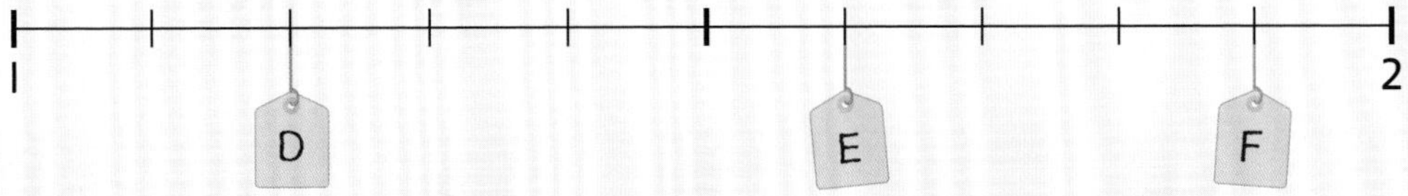
1
2
D
E
F

3
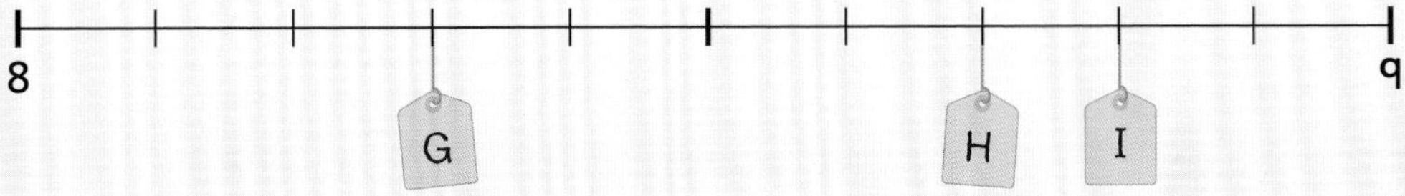
8
9
G
H
I

4
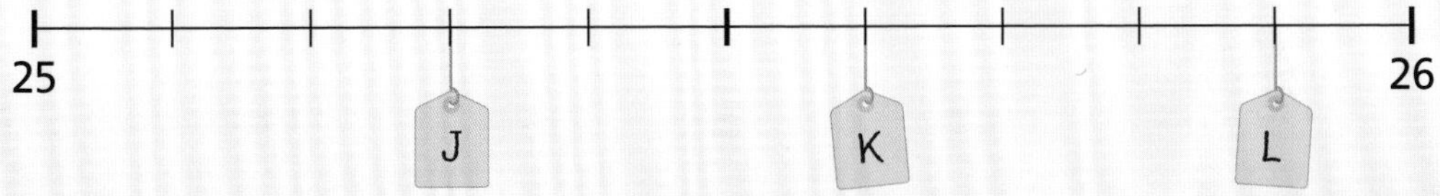
25
26
J
K
L

Complete these additions.

Use your bonds to help you.

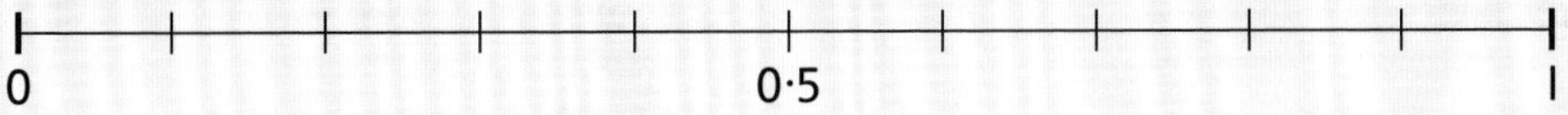
0
0·5
1

5 0·7 + ☐ = 1

6 0·6 + ☐ = 1

7 0·5 + ☐ = 1

8 3·6 + ☐ = 4

9 5·2 + ☐ = 6

10 7·3 + ☐ = 8

THINK What numbers are hidden on this line?

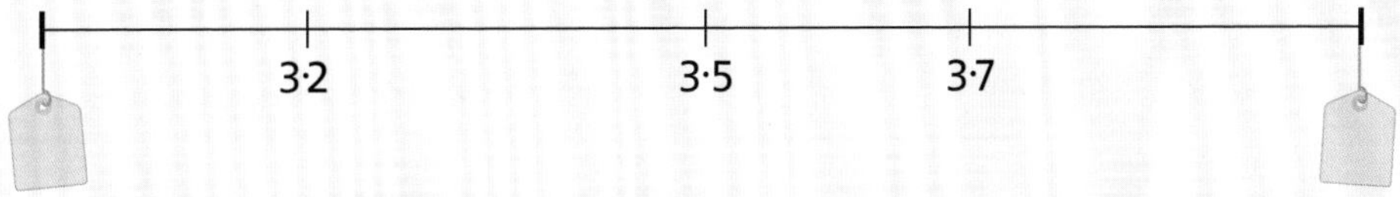
3·2
3·5
3·7

I am confident with placing 1-place decimals on a number line.

Write the numbers on the tags.

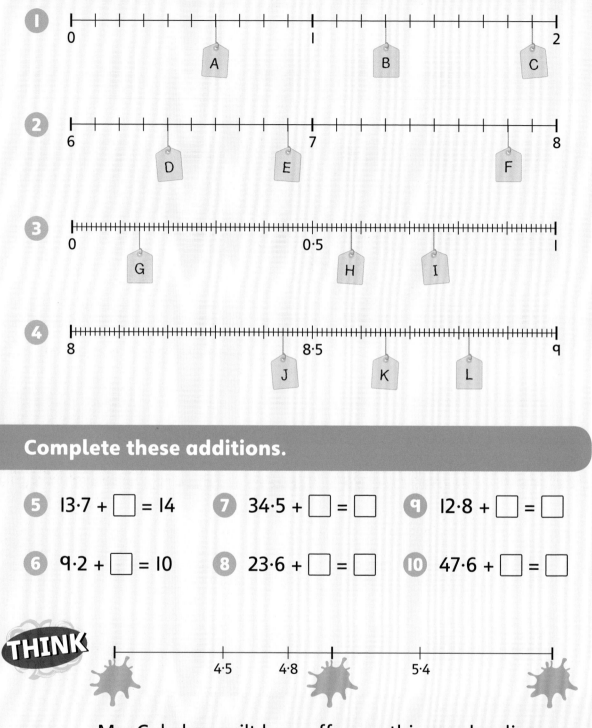

Complete these additions.

5 13·7 + ☐ = 14

7 34·5 + ☐ = ☐

9 12·8 + ☐ = ☐

6 9·2 + ☐ = 10

8 23·6 + ☐ = ☐

10 47·6 + ☐ = ☐

THINK

Mrs Cole has spilt her coffee on this number line.
Write what numbers are hidden by the coffee stains.

I am confident with placing 1- and 2-place decimals on a number line.

What is the value of each tag?

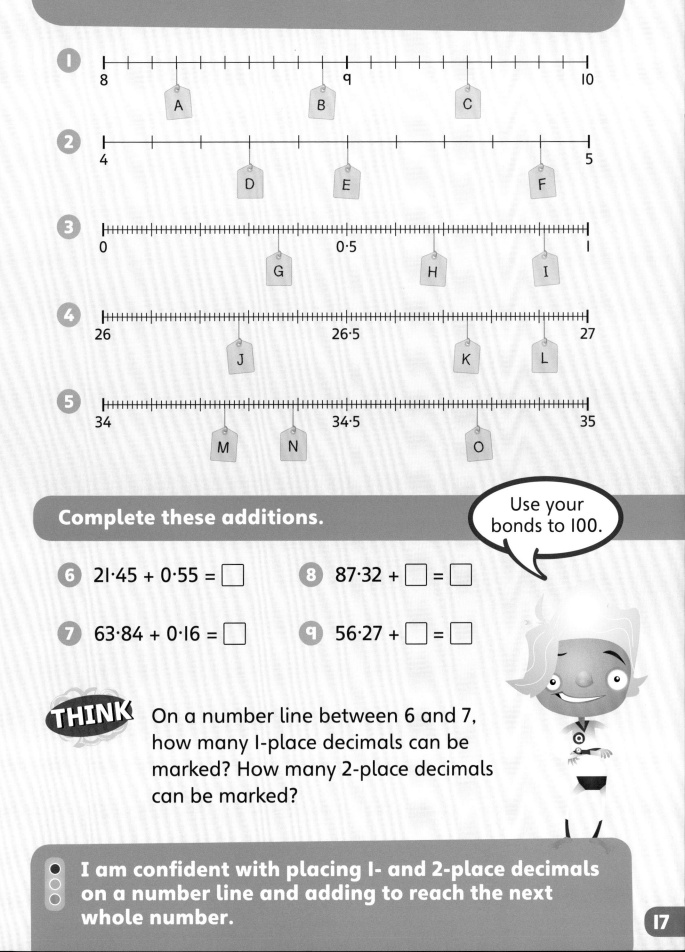

Complete these additions.

> Use your bonds to 100.

6. 21·45 + 0·55 = ☐

8. 87·32 + ☐ = ☐

7. 63·84 + 0·16 = ☐

9. 56·27 + ☐ = ☐

THINK On a number line between 6 and 7, how many 1-place decimals can be marked? How many 2-place decimals can be marked?

I am confident with placing 1- and 2-place decimals on a number line and adding to reach the next whole number.

Write the next four numbers in each sequence.

① 0·1, 0·2, 0·3, ☐, ☐, ☐, ☐   ⑤ 1·5, 1·6, 1·7, ☐, ☐, ☐, ☐

② 4·1, 4·2, 4·3, ☐, ☐, ☐, ☐   ⑥ 9·7, 9·6, 9·5, ☐, ☐, ☐, ☐

③ 6·3, 6·4, 6·5, ☐, ☐, ☐, ☐   ⑦ 8·8, 8·7, 8·6, ☐, ☐, ☐, ☐

④ 7·2, 7·3, 7·4, ☐, ☐, ☐, ☐   ⑧ 5·9, 5·8, 5·7, ☐, ☐, ☐, ☐

Answer these questions.

⑨ Which is the greater number, 3·4 or 4·3?

⑩ Which is the smaller number, 5·4 or 5·7?

⑪ Which is the greater number, 6·7 or 7·6?

⑫ Which is the smaller number, 0·4 or 2·0?

THINK Work with a partner and work out how many 1-place decimal numbers between 0 and 10 use the digit 9. Make sure you can demonstrate your total is correct. Convince each other. Convince your teacher.

I am confident with counting on in tenths and ordering 1-place decimals.

18

Write the next four numbers in each decimal sequence.

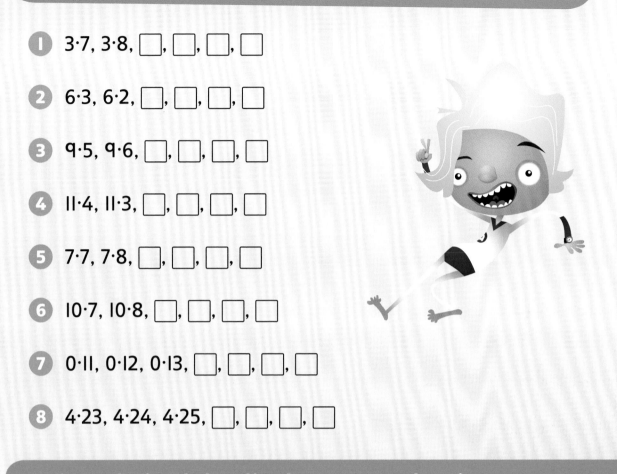

1. 3·7, 3·8, ☐, ☐, ☐, ☐

2. 6·3, 6·2, ☐, ☐, ☐, ☐

3. 9·5, 9·6, ☐, ☐, ☐, ☐

4. 11·4, 11·3, ☐, ☐, ☐, ☐

5. 7·7, 7·8, ☐, ☐, ☐, ☐

6. 10·7, 10·8, ☐, ☐, ☐, ☐

7. 0·11, 0·12, 0·13, ☐, ☐, ☐, ☐

8. 4·23, 4·24, 4·25, ☐, ☐, ☐, ☐

Write a decimal that lies between each pair.

9. 6·3   6·8

10. 8·8   9·3

11. 11·45   11·62

12. 25·34   25·43

THINK Work with a partner and together work out how many 1-place decimal numbers between 0 and 2 use the digit 9. Once you are certain, work out how many 2-place decimal numbers between 0 and 2 use the digit 9. Make sure you can demonstrate that your total is correct. Convince each other. Convince your teacher.

● I am confident with counting on in tenths
○ and hundredths.
○

Rounding decimals

> If the digit after the decimal point is 5 or greater, remember to round up.

Round these decimals to the nearest whole number.

1. 3·8
2. 6·2
3. 13·5
4. 27·9
5. 9·1
6. 17·4
7. 12·3
8. 1·4
9. 31·6
10. 22·6

Order these groups of three decimals from smallest to largest.

11. 3·6, 6·3, 2·3
12. 16·8, 18·6, 18·1
13. 1·9, 1·7, 1·1
14. 10·2, 10·9, 9·9
15. 3·8, 5·8, 9·3
16. 22·2, 21·7, 22·7

Write a 1-place decimal number between these pairs of numbers.

17. 13·6 and 15
18. 34·8 and 35·8
19. 27·1 and 27·9
20. 54·4 and 54·8
21. 81·1 and 81·6
22. 12·2 and 22·2

THINK Write seven different 1-place decimals that all round to 10. Which numbers round to 0?

○ **I am confident with rounding decimals to the nearest whole number.**

Round these decimals to the nearest whole number.

1. 63·7
2. 82·5
3. 19·1
4. 43·6

5. 14·6
6. 39·7
7. 62·5
8. 1·1

Write a decimal number between these pairs of numbers.

9. 13 and 14
10. 21·2 and 22

11. 54·1 and 54·5
12. 72·6 and 73

13. 11·1 and 11·6
14. 12·1 and 13

Solve these word problems.

15. Amir is buying cloth to make curtains. He needs 4·6 m of cloth but it is only sold in whole metres. How much cloth does he need to buy?

16. Flour is sold in kilogram bags. How many kilogram bags must the school cook buy if she needs 8·7 kg of flour?

17. Jackie needs 24·5 cm of ribbon to put around the edge of a wedding cake. She can only buy ribbon in whole centimetres. How much does she need to buy?

THINK How many 1-place decimal numbers round to 7? Is this the same as for 8? And for 1? And for 0?

I am confident with rounding decimals to the nearest whole number and finding 'in between' decimals.

Round these decimals to the nearest whole number.

1. 29·8
2. 16·5
3. 11·1
4. 64·6

5. 38·3
6. 7·61
7. 12·85
8. 90·14

9. 75·39
10. 42·55

Find a 2-place decimal number between these pairs of numbers.

11. 10·1 and 10·2
12. 72·6 and 74·1

13. 63·8 and 64
14. 92·2 and 92·4

15. 12·7 and 13
16. 54·5 and 54·9

Solve these word problems.

17. A builder needs 24·7 m of skirting board for a room. He can only buy a whole number of metres of skirting board. How much must he buy?

18. James has two partly-used bags of sand. One weighs 10·45 kg and the other weighs 15 kg. How much sand does he have in total?

19. A shop has 25·15 m of ribbon. Someone buys 10 m of it. How much is left?

THINK How many 2-place decimal numbers round to 7? Is this the same for 8? And for 1? And for 0?

I am confident with rounding decimals to the nearest whole number and finding 'in between' decimals.

11 and 12 times-tables

Complete these steps for the 11 times-table.

1. 4 × 10 = ☐   4 × 1 = ☐   so 4 × 11 = ☐

2. 8 × 10 = ☐   8 × 1 = ☐   so 8 × 11 = ☐

3. 11 × 10 = ☐   11 × 1 = ☐   so 11 × 11 = ☐

Complete these steps for the 12 times-table.

4. 3 × 10 = ☐   3 × 2 = ☐   so 3 × 12 = ☐

5. 7 × 10 = ☐   7 × 2 = ☐   so 7 × 12 = ☐

6. 6 × 10 = ☐   6 × 2 = ☐   so 6 × 12 = ☐

7. 9 × 10 = ☐   9 × 2 = ☐   so 9 × 12 = ☐

8. 12 × 10 = ☐   12 × 2 = ☐   so 12 × 12 = ☐

 Write three division facts using the 11 times-table.
Write three division facts using the 12 times-table.

○ **I am beginning to be confident with the 11 and 12 times-tables.**

23

Solve these multiplication problems.

1 $3 \times 11 = \Box$

2 $\Box \times 11 = 66$

3 $12 \times 11 = \Box$

4 $5 \times \Box = 55$

5 $11 \times 11 = \Box$

6 $\Box \times 11 = 99$

7 $\Box \times 11 = 22$

8 $\Box \times 11 = 110$

Complete these divisions.

9 $77 \div 11 = \Box$

10 $121 \div 11 = \Box$

11 $44 \div 11 = \Box$

12 $\Box \div 11 = 12$

13 $\Box \div 11 = 8$

14 $\Box \div 11 = 1$

Complete these multiplications.

15 $4 \times 12 = \Box$

16 $12 \times 12 = \Box$

17 $6 \times 12 = \Box$

18 $8 \times 12 = \Box$

19 $\Box \times 12 = 108$

20 $11 \times 12 = \Box$

21 $\Box \times 12 = 24$

22 $\Box \times 12 = 84$

23 $\Box \times 12 = 36$

Solve these division problems.

24 $108 \div 12 = \Box$

25 $\Box \div 12 = 12$

26 $72 \div 12 = \Box$

27 $96 \div 12 = \Box$

28 $\Box \div 12 = 5$

29 $36 \div 12 = \Box$

 Write out all the multiples of 12 up to 12 × 12. Look at the pattern in the ones. Which other times-table has the same unit pattern?

● **I am confident with the 11 and 12 times-tables.**

Mental and written multiplication

Use your mental strategies to answer
these multiplications.

1 3 × 36 = ☐

2 99 × 2 = ☐

3 23 × 4 = ☐

4 16 × 8 = ☐

5 7 × 52 = ☐

6 6 × 52 = ☐

7 6 × 24 = ☐

8 3 × 201 = ☐

9 2 × 299 = ☐

10 125 × 4 = ☐

11 5 × 120 = ☐

12 705 × 6 = ☐

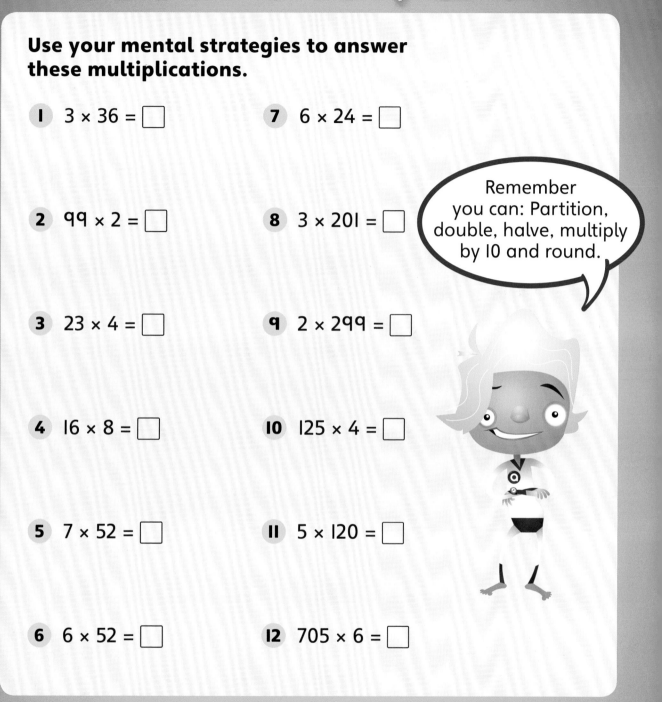

Remember
you can: Partition,
double, halve, multiply
by 10 and round.

 **THINK** Choose two calculations and explain
how you worked them out.

● I am confident with using mental strategies to
answer multiplication calculations.

Multiply a red number by a blue number to make a number on the grid. Use mental strategies to find all the numbers on the grid.

320	336	3216	102
192	256	170	150
2412	204	240	897

Red box:

3   4

5   6

7   8

Blue box:

64   34

402   25

48
    299

You can use your table knowledge to help you here.

THINK Write three multiplications. Each one should contain a 2-digit number and a 1-digit number. Neither number should be a multiple of 10 and each multiplication should have the same answer.

I am confident with using mental strategies to solve multiplications.

Choose how to work out these multiplications.

1 243 × 4 = ☐

2 3 × 420 = ☐

3 5 × 639 = ☐

4 4 × 827 = ☐

5 3 × 406 = ☐

6 9 × 134 = ☐

7 312 × 6 = ☐

8 498 × 8 = ☐

9 6 × 501 = ☐

10 8 × 202 = ☐

11 5 × 734 = ☐

12 7 × 342 = ☐

Solve these word problems.

13 If there are 365 days in a year, how many days in 3 years?

14 James has a shop that sells TVs. On one day he sells 4 TVs, each costing £578. How much money did the TVs cost altogether?

 **THINK** Did you need to use a written method to work out any of the answers? Write any you could do in your head.

I am confident with choosing the best method to answer multiplications.

Choose how to work out these multiplications.

1 $624 \times 6 = \square$

4 $967 \times 7 = \square$

2 $4 \times 808 = \square$

5 $203 \times 8 = \square$

3 $8 \times 234 = \square$

6 $7 \times 112 = \square$

Use a written method or mental strategy to answer these word problems. Show your workings.

7 Sanjeet pays £168 per year for broadband. How much does he pay for 3 years of broadband?

8 Each day a factory makes 205 cars. How many does it make in 7 days?

9 On a motorway there are 357 cars in a traffic jam. If each car has 4 people in it, how many people are stuck in the traffic jam?

10 Nick is laying paving slabs to make a long drive to a house. He lays 8 slabs in each row and lays 182 rows. How many slabs does he use in total?

THINK What are the missing digits in $\square\,9\,\square \times 6 = 1794$?

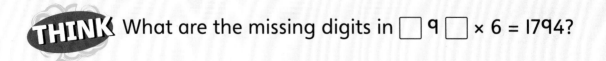

● I am confident with choosing the best method to
perform a multiplication.

Multiplying and dividing

Work out the missing inputs and outputs for these function machines.

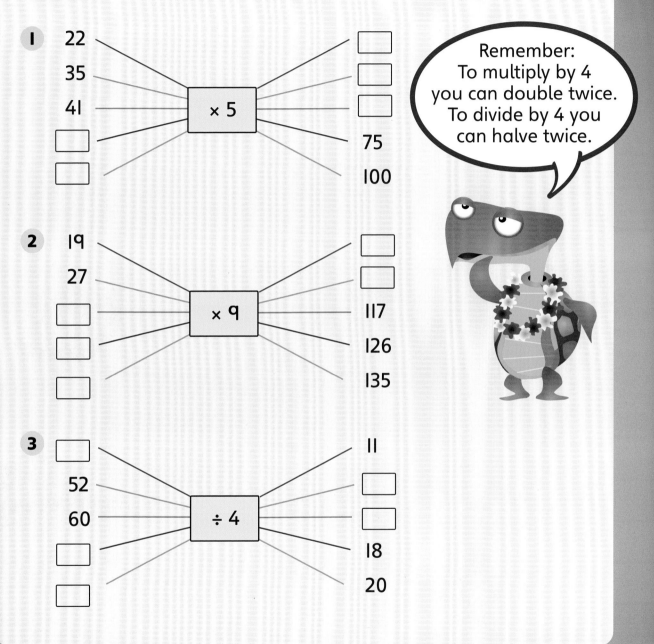

1
22
35
41
☐
☐

× 5

☐
☐
☐
75
100

Remember:
To multiply by 4
you can double twice.
To divide by 4 you
can halve twice.

2
19
27
☐
☐
☐

× 9

☐
☐
117
126
135

3
☐
52
60
☐
☐

÷ 4

11
☐
☐
18
20

THINK The output is 120. If the function machine is multiplying by a 1-digit number, what could the input and function be?

● I am confident with multiplying and dividing by
○ 4, 5 and 9.

Work out the missing inputs and outputs.

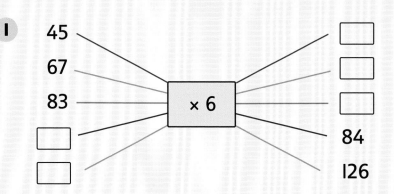

1

45
67
83
[ ]
[ ]

× 6

[ ]
[ ]
[ ]
84
126

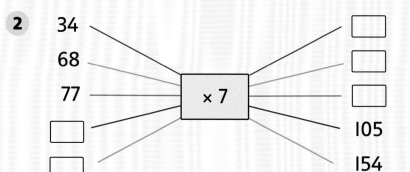

2

34
68
77
[ ]
[ ]

× 7

[ ]
[ ]
[ ]
105
154

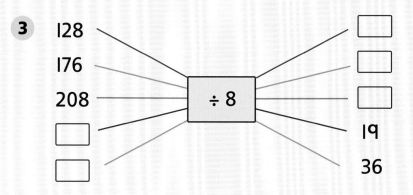

3

128
176
208
[ ]
[ ]

÷ 8

[ ]
[ ]
[ ]
19
36

 **THINK** The output is 144 and the input is an even number. The function is × something, where the 'something' is an odd number less than 10. What could the possible inputs and functions be?

- I am confident with multiplying and dividing 2-digit numbers.

calculating area and perimeter

Calculate the area of each shape.

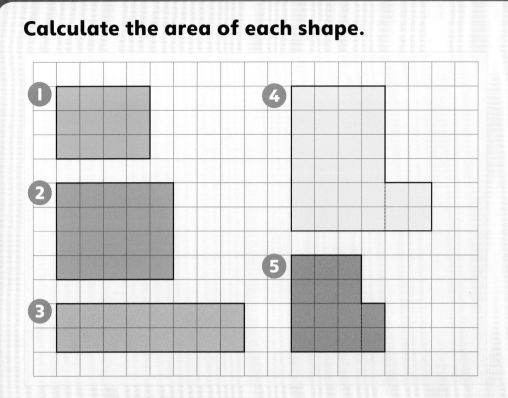

Use multiplication to find the areas of these allotments.

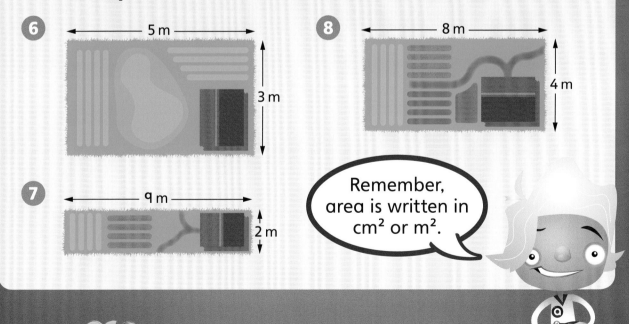

Remember, area is written in cm² or m².

THINK Can you work out the perimeter of the first rectangle on the page?

I am confident with calculating the area of rectangles and 'L' shapes by adding or multiplying.

Calculate the area of each shape.

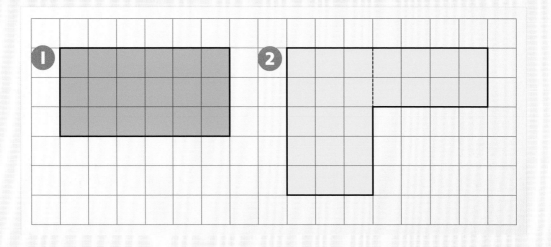

Use multiplication to find the areas of these allotments.

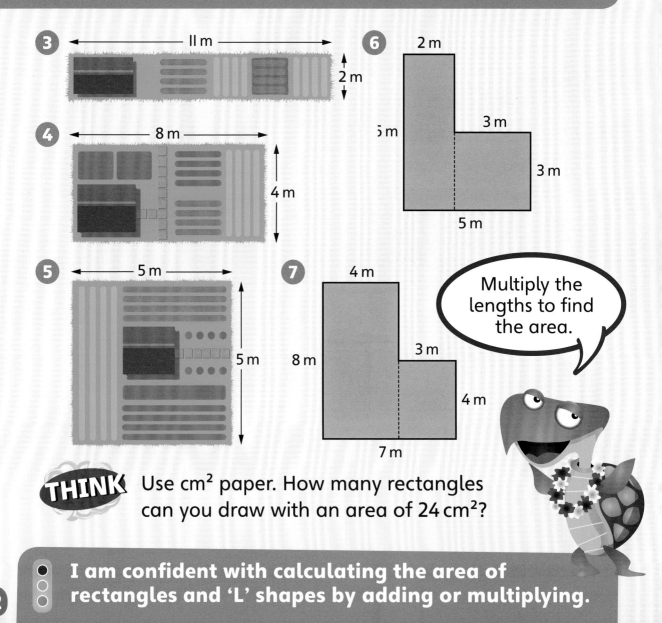

③ ← 11 m → 2 m

④ ← 8 m → 4 m

⑤ ← 5 m → 5 m

⑥ 2 m, 3 m, 5 m, 3 m, 5 m

⑦ 4 m, 8 m, 3 m, 4 m, 7 m

Multiply the lengths to find the area.

THINK Use cm² paper. How many rectangles can you draw with an area of 24 cm²?

I am confident with calculating the area of rectangles and 'L' shapes by adding or multiplying.

Calculate the area and perimeter of each shape.

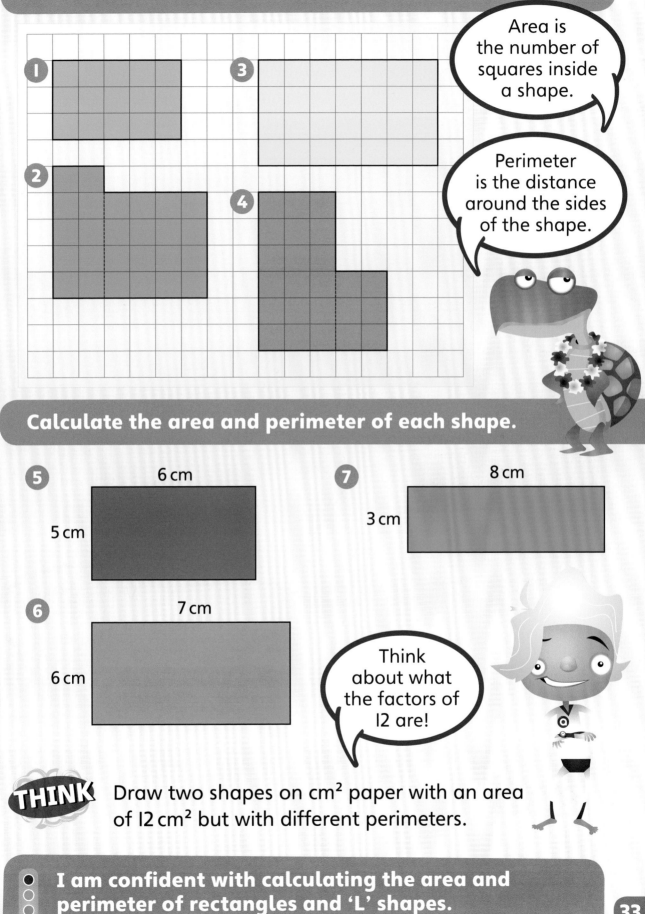

Area is the number of squares inside a shape.

Perimeter is the distance around the sides of the shape.

Calculate the area and perimeter of each shape.

5

6 cm

5 cm

7

8 cm

3 cm

6

7 cm

6 cm

Think about what the factors of 12 are!

THINK Draw two shapes on cm² paper with an area of 12 cm² but with different perimeters.

○ I am confident with calculating the area and
○
○ perimeter of rectangles and 'L' shapes.

33

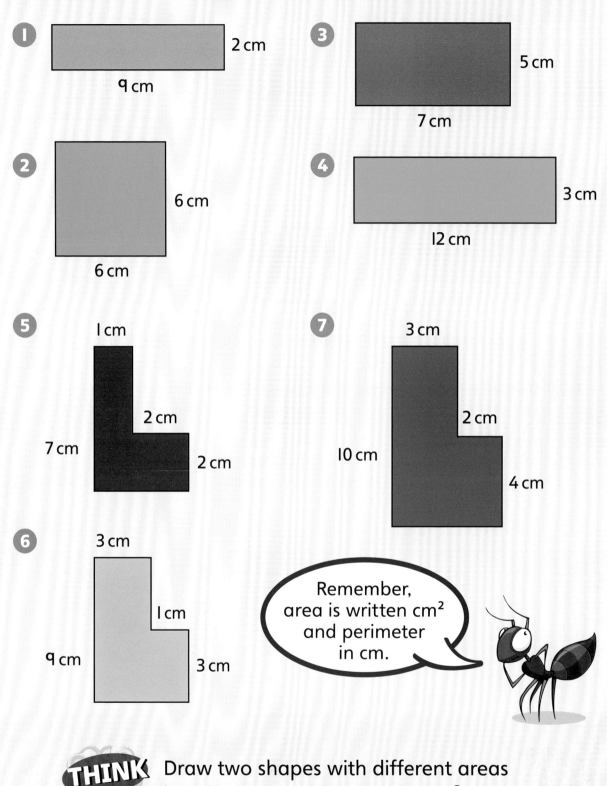

1 2 cm 9 cm

2 6 cm 6 cm

3 5 cm 7 cm

4 3 cm 12 cm

5 1 cm 2 cm 7 cm 2 cm

6 3 cm 1 cm 9 cm 3 cm

7 3 cm 2 cm 10 cm 4 cm

Remember, area is written cm² and perimeter in cm.

THINK Draw two shapes with different areas but the same perimeter. Use cm² paper.

I am confident with calculating the area and perimeter of rectangles and 'L' shapes.

Properties of 2D and 3D Shapes

Name and describe each triangle. Use the labels to help.

> Shape a is a scalene triangle. It has no equal angles and is not symmetrical. This one has one right angle.

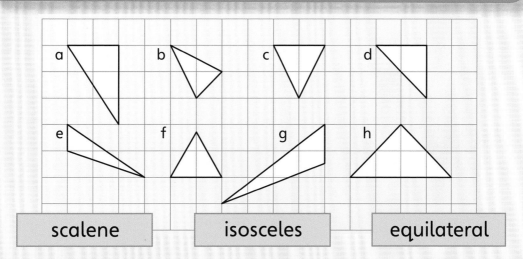

| scalene | isosceles | equilateral |

Name and describe each quadrilateral.

> Shape i is a rhombus. The diagonally opposite angles are equal and all sides are the same length.

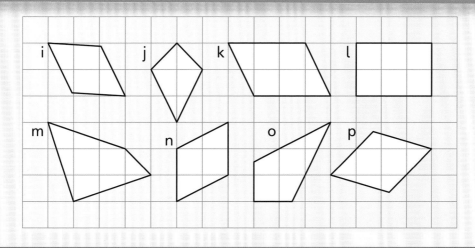

THINK Take a piece of paper. Fold it. Cut a shape out of the folded side so that when you open the piece of paper, you see a hole which is an equilateral triangle.

⦿ **I am confident with naming and describing the**
○ **properties of triangles and quadrilaterals.**
○

Name and describe each 3D shape. Say how many faces, vertices and edges it has. Then describe the 2D faces of each shape.

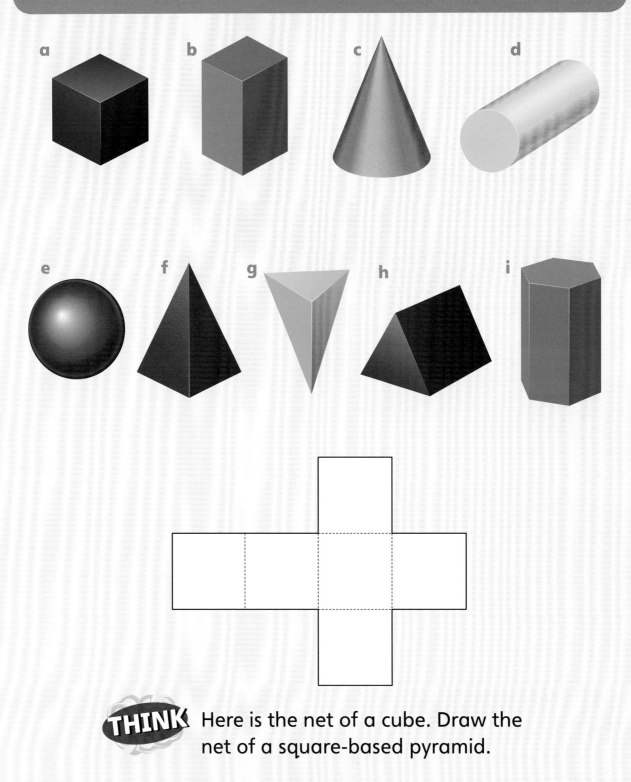

a

b

c

d

e

f

g

h

i

THINK Here is the net of a cube. Draw the net of a square-based pyramid.

I am confident with naming and describing the properties of 3D shapes.

Complete the table. Use solid shapes to help you.

1

Polyhedron	Faces	Vertices	Edges
Tetrahedron			
Square-based pyramid			
Cuboid			
Triangular prism			
Hexagonal prism			
Hexagon-based pyramid			

Euler's special number
Add the faces and the vertices. Subtract the edges.

Euler was a famous Swiss mathematician who was born in 1707.

Name the mystery shapes.

2 It has 4 faces, 4 vertices and 6 edges.

3 It has 6 faces, 12 edges and 8 vertices.

True or false?

4 A cone is not a polyhedron.

5 A triangular prism has more faces than a cube.

6 A cuboid has the same number of edges as a cube.

7 A hexagonal prism has the same number of vertices as a hexagon-based prism.

I am confident with the properties of 3D shapes, including the number of faces, edges and vertices.

Decimal numbers in length

Copy the lines. Write lengths as metres and centimetres above the line and as metres below the line.

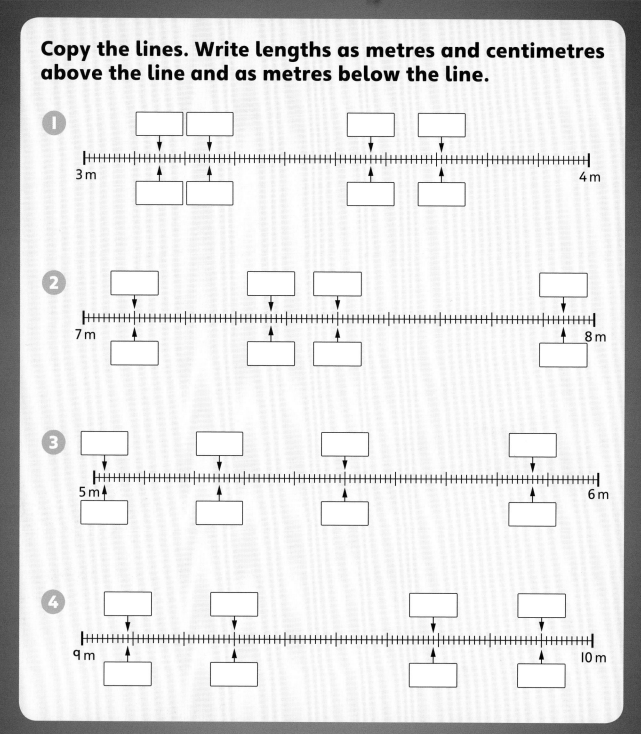

THINK Draw a line from 4 to 5 and mark three numbers with two decimal places.

○ **I am confident with writing lengths in metres, and in**
○ **metres and centimetres.**
○

Write these lengths in metres.

1. 2 m 34 cm

2. 2 m 40 cm

3. 5 m 62 cm

4. 7 m 39 cm

5. 8 m 60 cm

6. 4 m 11 cm

Write these lengths in metres and centimetres.

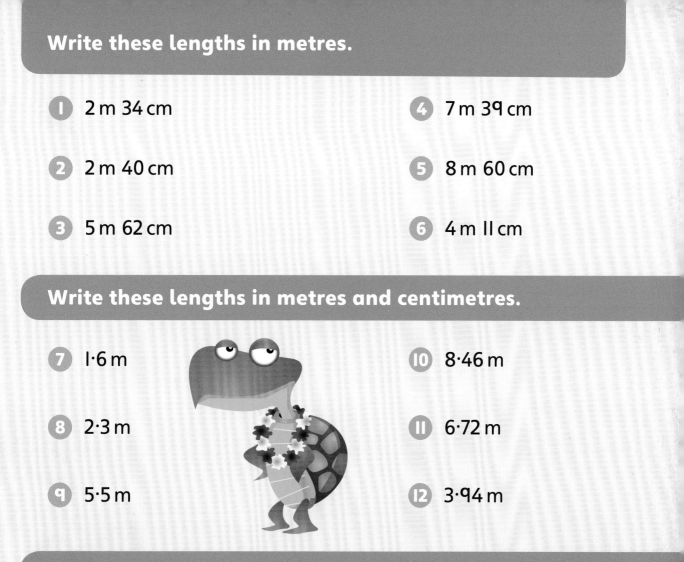

7. 1·6 m

8. 2·3 m

9. 5·5 m

10. 8·46 m

11. 6·72 m

12. 3·94 m

Copy this line and mark these measurements on it.

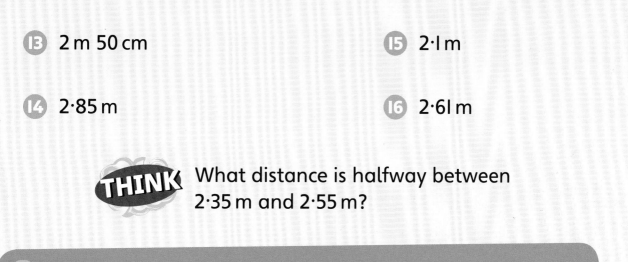

2 m   3 m

13. 2 m 50 cm

14. 2·85 m

15. 2·1 m

16. 2·61 m

THINK What distance is halfway between 2·35 m and 2·55 m?

○ **I am confident with writing lengths in metres, and in metres and centimetres.**

Write the lengths of these animals in order from the shortest to the longest.

1

1·48 m

1·25 m

1·34 m

2

3·76 m

2·55 m

3·16 m

3

3·77 m

3·98 m

3·76 m

4

2·19 m

2·81 m

2·01 m

 THINK Draw an animal longer than 0·5 m and less than 0·6 m. Mark its length in metres.

○●○○ I am confident with ordering lengths with two decimal places.

Here are the results of a long jump competition. Write the three jumps for each person in order, from shortest to longest.

Name	Jump 1	Jump 2	Jump 3
Sara	3·61 m	3·58 m	3·65 m
Michael	4·42 m	3·98 m	4·37 m
Imran	4·88 m	4·64 m	4·92 m
Kenji	5·23 m	5·15 m	5·31 m
Sherin	3·82 m	3·76 m	3·99 m
Zoya	5·79 m	5·24 m	5·6 m
Peter	4·1 m	4·25 m	4·39 m
Mia	3·43 m	3·5 m	3·58 m

 THINK Ben thinks that 3·4 m is a shorter length than 3·04 m. Write a sentence to explain to Ben why this is not right.

○ **I am confident with ordering lengths with two decimal places.**

Compare the distances on each sign post. Which is the longer distance?

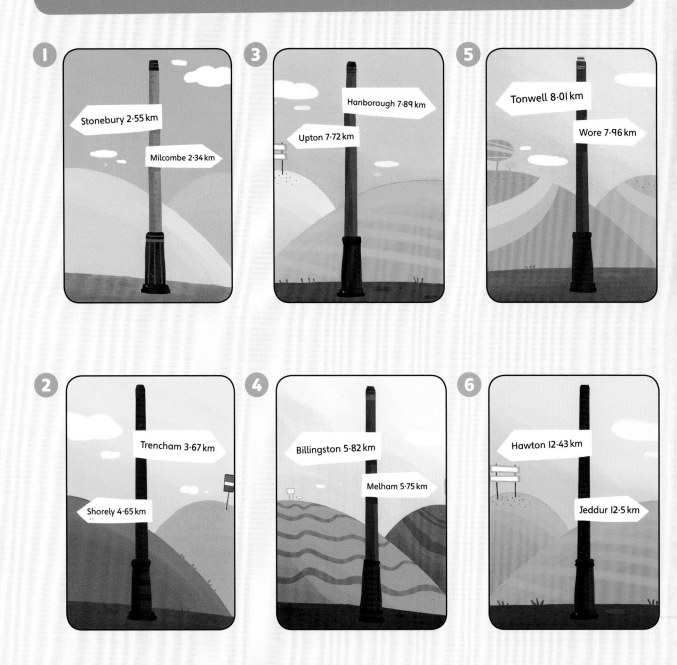

1
Stonebury 2·55 km
Milcombe 2·34 km

3
Hanborough 7·89 km
Upton 7·72 km

5
Tonwell 8·01 km
Wore 7·96 km

2
Trencham 3·67 km
Shorely 4·65 km

4
Billingston 5·82 km
Melham 5·75 km

6
Hawton 12·43 km
Jeddur 12·5 km

THINK Draw a number line to show all the 1- and 2-place decimal numbers that come between 0·5 and 0·66. Which number is half-way between these two?

I am confident with comparing lengths with two decimal places.

Equivalent fractions and decimals

$$\frac{3}{6} = \frac{5}{10}$$

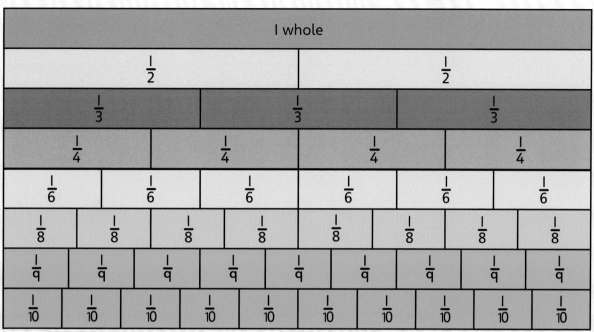

Write at least one fraction that is the same size as:

1 $\frac{1}{2}$

2 $\frac{1}{3}$

3 $\frac{1}{4}$

4 $\frac{2}{10}$

5 $\frac{4}{6}$

6 $\frac{6}{8}$

Write what needs to be added to each of these fractions to make 1 whole.

7 $\frac{2}{5}$

8 $\frac{5}{8}$

9 $\frac{1}{3}$

10 $\frac{1}{6}$

11 $\frac{3}{10}$

12 $\frac{4}{5}$

 **THINK** Write three fractions with a total of 1. Do this two more times with different fractions each time.

○ **I am confident with equivalent fractions and**
○ **adding to a fraction to make a whole number.**

Write the fraction of the coloured part of each square.

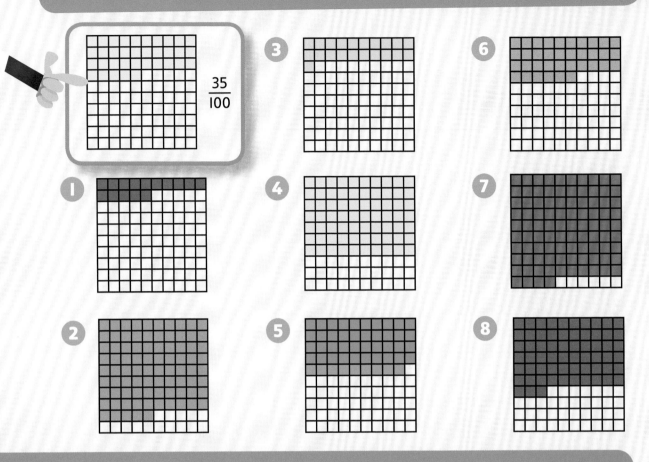

$\dfrac{35}{100}$

For each square also write the coloured fraction as a decimal.

$\dfrac{35}{100} = 0{\cdot}35$

Write each fraction as a number of hundredths. Use a 10 × 10 square to help you.

9 one-half

10 one-quarter

11 one-tenth

12 three-quarters

13 seven-tenths

14 three-tenths

THINK Seven-tenths lies between 50 and 80 hundredths. Can you find some other fractions that lie between this number of hundredths?

I am confident with writing hundredths as fractions and decimals.

Solve these problems.

> Change the fractions to decimals to help you work out the answers.

1. There is $2\frac{1}{2}$ m of ribbon. 30 cm is cut off. How much ribbon is left?

2. James is $1\frac{1}{4}$ m tall. His sister is 15 cm taller than James. How tall is his sister?

3. A male elephant is $3\frac{3}{4}$ m tall. A female elephant is 60 cm smaller than it. How tall is the female elephant?

4. A wall is 2·85 m tall. Gabi puts a picture hook $\frac{1}{2}$ m from the top of the wall. How high up the wall is the hook?

5. In July a sunflower is $1\frac{1}{2}$ m tall. By August it has grown 60 cm taller. How tall is it in August?

6. A hedge is 3·62 m tall. Mike cuts $\frac{1}{2}$ m from the top of the hedge. How tall is the hedge now?

THINK What length in centimetres can Katie cut five times from her 5 m ribbon to leave exactly 4 m? What if she wants to leave 3 m?

Solve these problems.

> Change the fractions to decimals to help you work out the answers.

1. Kim's garage is 5 m 35 cm long. The length of Kim's car is $4\frac{1}{4}$ m. How much shorter is the car than the garage?

2. An adult giraffe is $5\frac{3}{4}$ m tall. A baby giraffe is 1·75 m tall. How much taller is the adult giraffe than the baby?

3. A plank of wood is 3·1 m long. Gabi cuts off $\frac{1}{2}$ m from it. How long is the plank now?

4. Sam is 1·9 m tall. His brother is $\frac{1}{4}$ m taller than Sam. How tall is his brother?

5. Claire buys 4·25 m of wire. She cuts off a $1\frac{3}{4}$ m length from it. How much is left?

6. Amy has two lengths of string. One is 2·7 m and the other is $2\frac{3}{10}$ m. What is the total length of string that Amy has?

7. Sarah has 7 pieces of ribbon, each 30 cm long. What is the total length of the ribbon? Give your answer in metres.

THINK What length in centimetres can Tom cut four times from his 5 m string to leave exactly 2 m?

○ **I am confident with converting between fraction and decimal hundredths.**

Adding 2-, 3- and 4-digit numbers

Complete these addition patterns using mental methods.

1.
38 + 45 = ☐
338 + 45 = ☐
3238 + 45 = ☐

4.
19 + 79 = ☐
819 + 79 = ☐
6319 + 79 = ☐

2.
62 + 29 = ☐
862 + 29 = ☐
9562 + 29 = ☐

5.
45 + 48 = ☐
745 + 48 = ☐
7445 + 48 = ☐

3.
54 + 37 = ☐
654 + 37 = ☐
8254 + 37 = ☐

6.
36 + 58 = ☐
636 + 58 = ☐
9036 + 58 = ☐

Solve these word problems using mental methods.

7. A factory outlet sells microwave ovens. It has 235 ovens in stock. A delivery of 57 more ovens arrives. How many ovens do they have in total now?

8. James has two money boxes. In one is £29 and in the other is £49. James takes all this money and pays it into his bank account. If he had £573 in the account already, how much did he have in the account after paying the money in?

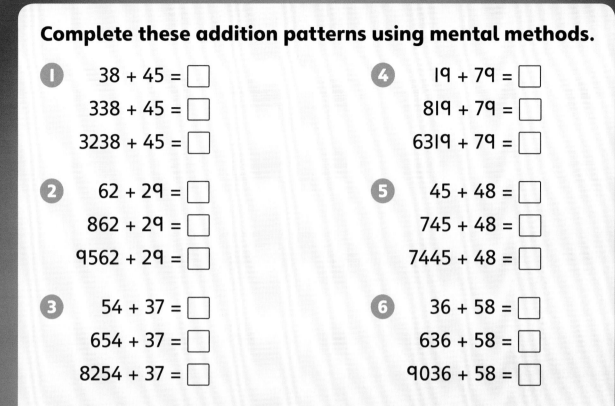

THINK Two 2-digit numbers AB + CD make 91. If you add all of the digits A + B + C + D, you get 19 (the reverse of 91). What could the numbers be?

I am confident with mental addition of 2-, 3- and 4- digit numbers.

Complete these additions using mental strategies.

① 67 + 85 = ☐

② 114 + 87 = ☐

③ 3045 + 76 = ☐

④ 846 + 46 = ☐

⑤ 8417 + 66 = ☐

⑥ 374 + 81 = ☐

⑦ 733 + 47 = ☐

⑧ 8575 + 64 = ☐

⑨ 853 + 83 = ☐

⑩ 7543 + 28 = ☐

⑪ 2649 + 74 = ☐

⑫ 758 + 67 = ☐

Solve these word problems using mental methods.

⑬ Twin sisters, Claire and Molly, each raise some money for charity. Claire raises £38 by doing a sponsored walk and Molly raises £44 by doing a sponsored spell. Other children in their class have also raised £325. Claire's and Molly's money is added to this. What is the total now?

⑭ Class M has 28 children and Class B has 33 children. In the rest of the school (not counting classes M and B) there are 184 children. How many children are in the whole school?

 Two 2-digit numbers AB + CD make 81. If you add all the digits A + B + C + D, you get 18 (the reverse of 81). What could the numbers be?

○ I am confident with mental addition of 2-, 3- and
○ 4-digit numbers.
○

Subtracting 3- and 4-digit numbers

Complete these subtractions by counting up.

1 400 – 348 = ☐

4 900 – 847 = ☐

2 800 – 726 = ☐

5 200 – 119 = ☐

3 500 – 427 = ☐

6 700 – 638 = ☐

303 – 165 =

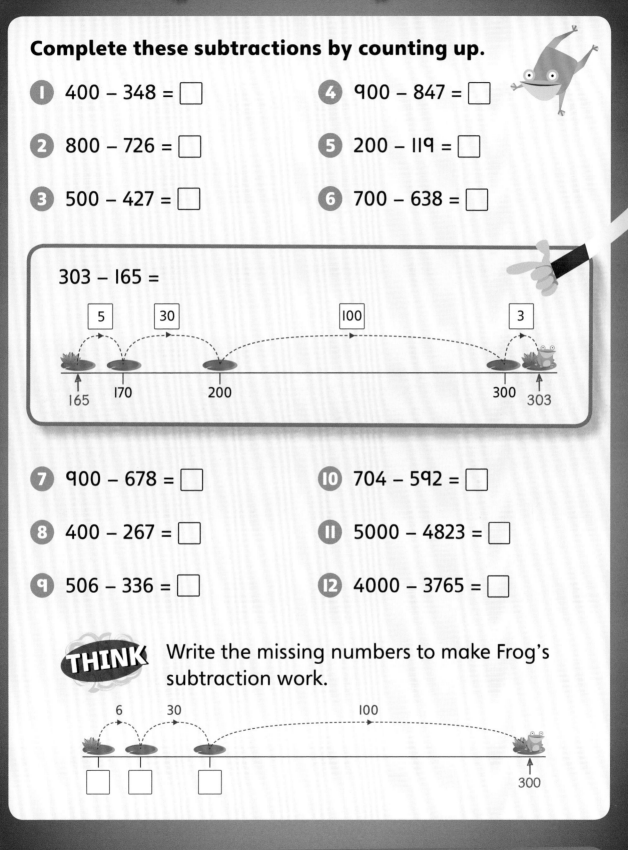

7 900 – 678 = ☐

10 704 – 592 = ☐

8 400 – 267 = ☐

11 5000 – 4823 = ☐

9 506 – 336 = ☐

12 4000 – 3765 = ☐

THINK Write the missing numbers to make Frog's subtraction work.

I am confident with subtracting 3- and 4-digit numbers using the method of counting up.

49

Complete these subtractions.

1. $406 - 263 = \square$
2. $305 - 127 = \square$
3. $702 - 588 = \square$
4. $804 - 652 = \square$
5. $6000 - 5373 = \square$
6. $8004 - 7467 = \square$

7. $9003 - 8874 = \square$
8. $7006 - 6439 = \square$
9. $7005 - 3584 = \square$
10. $6002 - 4826 = \square$
11. $8007 - 2758 = \square$
12. $9010 - 6337 = \square$

Solve these word problems.

13. Claire and Mark are planning their honeymoon. The original price was £2500 but they found an offer online for £490 off. They have saved £1380 so far. How much more money do they need?

14. Gopal and Zuri climbed 167 m of a 405 m climbing wall. How far away were they from the top?

15. Hannah's hockey team celebrated their 500th match! Hannah has played 246 matches with the team. How many have the team played without Hannah?

THINK In a subtraction, Frog makes three jumps to reach 1000. The first jump is a 1-digit number, the second is a multiple of 10 and the third is a multiple of 100. Each jump has the same initial digit. What could the subtraction be?

 **I am confident with subtracting 3- and 4-digit numbers using the method of counting up.**

using factors to multiply

Copy and complete these multiplications.

1. $36 \times \square = 144$

2. $\square \times 24 = 192$

3. $52 \times \square = 416$

4. $138 \div 6 = \square$

5. $184 \div 8 = \square$

6. $\square \times 24 = 288$

7. $48 \times \square = 192$

8. $32 \times \square = 192$

Solve these word problems.

9. A pack of playing cards has 52 cards. How many cards are there in 4 packs?

10. How many eggs in 37 boxes of 6 eggs?

11. A dozen is 12. How many is 24 dozen?

12. The perimeter of a square is 136 cm. What is the length of each side?

13. The perimeter of a regular octagon is 128 cm. What is the length of each side?

 **THINK** Divide 288 by 2, by 4, by 6, by 8 and by 12. Can you write 288 as the answer to a multiplication question that uses only the numbers 2 and 3 and the × sign?

○
○ **I am confident with using factors to solve**
○ **multiplication problems.**

Scaling

Copy rectangle a on to centimetre squared paper.

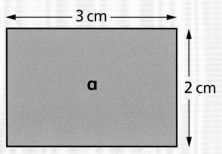

1. Count the squares to find the area and write it down.

2. Draw another rectangle, b, with sides double the length of rectangle a. Count the squares to find the area and write it down.

3. Draw another rectangle, c, with sides three times the length of rectangle a. Find the area and write it down.

4. Draw another rectangle, d, with sides four times the length of rectangle a. Find the area and write it down.

5. Divide the area of rectangle b by the area of rectangle a. How many times does it go?

6. Divide the area of rectangle c by the area of rectangle a. How many times does it go?

7. Divide the area of rectangle d by the area of rectangle a. How many times does it go?

8. Write a rule for what happens to the area if you multiply the sides of a rectangle by 2, by 3 and by 4.

I am confident with scaling using mental multiplication strategies.

Answer these questions.

Find the areas using mental multiplication.

1 Work out the area of the following rectangles.

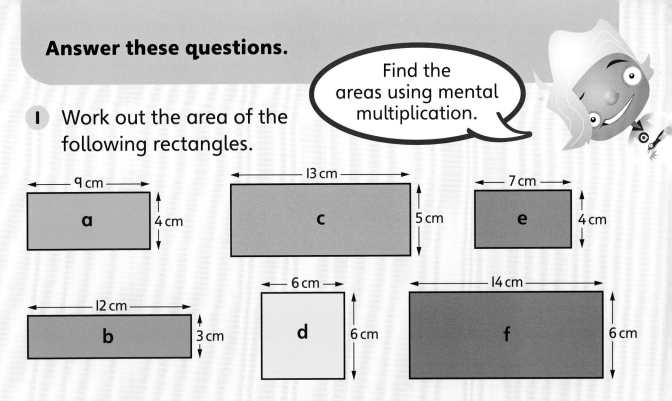

2 Double the sides of each rectangle and write the new area.

Use your answers to copy and complete the table below and answer the questions.

Rectangle	Area	Area of rectangle with sides doubled
a	36 cm²	144 cm²
b		
c		
d		
e		
f		

3 Compare the two areas for each rectangle. How much larger is the area of the rectangle with sides doubled?

4 Write a rule for what happens to the area of a rectangle when you double the sides. Test your rule on at least two new rectangles.

● I am confident with scaling using mental multiplication strategies.

Answer these questions.

1 Work out the area of the following rectangles.

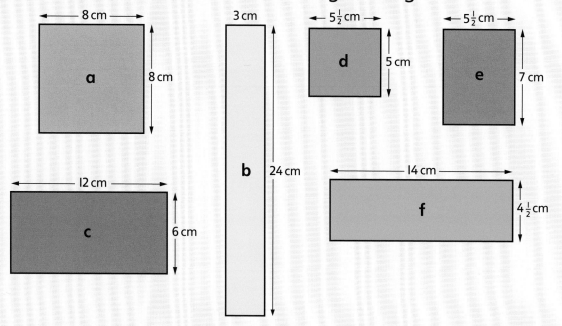

a — 8 cm × 8 cm

b — 3 cm × 24 cm

c — 12 cm × 6 cm

d — $5\frac{1}{2}$ cm × 5 cm

e — $5\frac{1}{2}$ cm × 7 cm

f — 14 cm × $4\frac{1}{2}$ cm

2 Double the sides of each rectangle and write the new area.

Use your answers to copy and complete the table below and answer the questions.

Rectangle	Area	Area of rectangle with sides doubled
a		
b		
c		

3 Write a rule for how many times bigger the area gets when you double the sides of a rectangle.

 **THINK** Calculate the area of this shape. Double each side and calculate the new area. Does your rule work for this shape?

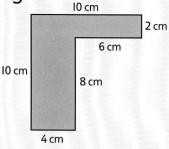

10 cm · 2 cm · 6 cm · 10 cm · 8 cm · 4 cm

● I am confident with scaling using mental
● multiplication strategies.

Factorial function

1 Choose two different counters. How many different ways can you arrange them?

2 Choose three different counters to represent these. Label them A, B and C.

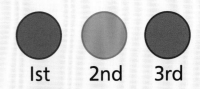

Ist 2nd 3rd

3 Place A in the Ist place above. Work out how many arrangements there are if A stays put and you only move B and C. Write down each arrangement.

4 Now place B in the Ist place and move A and C. Write down each arrangement you can make.

5 Now you have tried all the possible arrangements with A and B in the Ist place. Place C in the Ist place and repeat the process.

6 How many arrangements have you found in total?

Copy and complete the table below.

The number of possible arrangements could be found like this:

2 counters – 2 × 1 = 2

3 counters – 3 × 2 × 1 = 6

4 counters – 4 × 3 × 2 × 1 = ☐

5 counters – 5 × 4 × 3 × 2 × 1 = ☐

Number of counters	Number of arrangements
2	
3	
4	
5	120
6	720

THINK Check if 5 and 6 work to give I20 and 720.

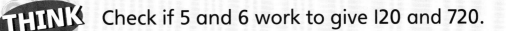

I am confident with finding out how many ways a number of items can be arranged.

55

Choose four different counters to represent these. Label them A, B, C and D.

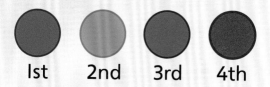

Ist   2nd   3rd   4th

1   Place A in the Ist place above and B in the 2nd place. Record possible arrangements of the four counters if you only move C and D.

2   Keep A in the Ist place and swap B with C so C is in the 2nd place. Repeat the process above, recording each arrangement.

3   Keep A in the Ist place and swap C with D so D is in the 2nd place. Record each possible arrangement.

4   Now you have tried all possible arrangements with A in the Ist place, repeat the approach with B in the Ist place. Record the same number of arrangements.

5   Now find the rest of the possible arrangements with C in the Ist place and then with D in the Ist place.

6   How many arrangements are there in total?

7   Copy and complete this table.

Number of counters	Number of arrangements	Pattern for number of arrangements
2		2 × 1
3	6	3 × 2 × 1
4		4 × 3 × 2 × 1
5	120	
6	720	

8   What do you notice about the pattern in column 3? Can you check whether the pattern works if you continue it?

● I am confident with finding out how many ways a number of items can be arranged.

Work out the number of possible arrangements in a line for:

It is easiest to keep A and B in place and then try possible arrangements of the other two. Then swap the first two around and repeat.

1 2 objects.

2 4 objects. Label 4 objects A, B, C and D.

3 Can you show that you have definitely found them all? Copy and begin to complete this table.

Number of objects	Number of arrangements
2	
3	6
4	
5	
6	
7	

4 Look at the numbers in the second column. Can 2, 3 and 4 be worked out as shown below?

2 objects: 2 × 1 = ☐

3 objects: 3 × 2 × 1 = ☐

4 objects: 4 × 3 × 2 × 1 = ☐

How could you quickly work out the number of arrangements for 6 objects?

5 Continue this pattern to find and fill in the number of possible arrangements for 5 and 6 objects.

THINK Find how many ways you could arrange 7 objects.

● I am confident with finding out how many
● ways a number of items can be arranged.
●

Adding 4-digit numbers

$3164 + 2553 = \square$

3000	100	60	4
+ 2000	500	50	3
	100		
5000	700	10	7 = 5717

Complete these additions.

1 $2352 + 1575 = \square$

2000	300	50	2
+ 1000	500	70	5

3 $6229 + 3525 = \square$

6000	200	20	9
+ 3000	500	20	5

2 $4824 + 4431 = \square$

4000	800	20	4
+ 4000	400	30	1

4 $4637 + 2654 = \square$

4000	600	30	7
+ 2000	600	50	4

Now try these.

5
```
  3525
+ 1183
_____
```

7
```
  5745
+ 3717
_____
```

6
```
  6342
+ 1857
_____
```

8
```
  3268
+ 2348
_____
```

THINK What could the missing digits be?

```
    3 □ 6 2
+   □ 4 □ 8
        1
_____
  □ 2 9 0
```

○
○ **I am confident with adding 4-digit numbers using**
○ **the column method.**

Complete these additions using column addition.

1 4756 + 3862 = ☐

7 235 + 953 + 864 = ☐

2 6846 + 517 = ☐

8 629 + 957 + 47 = ☐

3 361 + 872 + 685 = ☐

9 319 + 208 + 425 = ☐

4 6446 + 1178 = ☐

10 26 + 57 + 27 + 31 = ☐

5 9364 + 477 = ☐

11 839 + 314 + 18 = ☐

6 78 + 38 + 67 + 49 = ☐

12 3856 + 2918 = ☐

Solve this word problem.

13 James, Kate and Freya raise some money for charity. James raises £285, Kate raises £482 and Freya raises £328. How much do they raise altogether?

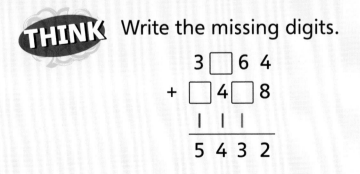

THINK Write the missing digits.

```
    3 ☐ 6 4
  + ☐ 4 ☐ 8
    1 1 1
  ─────────
    5 4 3 2
```

I am confident with adding 2-digit, 3-digit and 4-digit numbers.

Adding money

Complete these additions using column addition.

1 £24·82 + £41·56 = ☐

5 £32·14 + £29·48 = ☐

2 £54·29 + £32·48 = ☐

6 £52·99 + £36·67 = ☐

3 £77·22 + £13·61 = ☐

7 £48·52 + £37·57 = ☐

4 £48·26 + £36·39 = ☐

8 £46·69 + £27·68 = ☐

Solve these problems.

9 Rufus buys a jumper costing £44·52 and a T-shirt costing £11·29. How much did his items cost altogether?

10 Jess wants to buy a pair of shorts costing £13·89 and a vest top costing £6·49. She has £20. How much more money does she need to buy them?

THINK Write three items of clothing that add to £10. None of the items is an exact number of pounds.

○
○ **I am confident with adding money amounts using**
○ **column addition.**

Find the cost of:

1. the pair of trousers and the shirt.
2. the dress and the hat.
3. the coat and the umbrella.
4. the pair of trousers and the T-shirt.
5. the coat, the hat and the handbag.
6. the coat, the shirt and the umbrella.

Solve this problem.

7. Kim has a £20 note and £17·78 in change in her purse. She buys a jacket costing £25·49 and a pair of trousers costing £12·23. How much money does she have left now?

THINK   Write the prices of three items that would have a total cost of £12·12. No prices should be whole numbers of pounds.

○
○ **I am confident with adding money amounts using**
○ **column addition.**

Subtracting 3- and 4-digit numbers

Answer the subtractions. Use the expanded method.

1 2579 – 377 = ☐

2000	500	70	9
–	300	70	7

2 6579 – 2424 = ☐

6000	500	70	9
– 2000	400	20	4

3 4866 – 525 = ☐

4000	800	60	6
–	500	20	5

4 4637 – 1282 = ☐

4000	600	30	7
– 1000	200	80	2

Use the compact method.

5 3595 – 1183 = ☐

```
  3595
– 1183
_____
```

6 6937 – 4606 = ☐

```
  6937
– 4606
_____
```

7 5749 – 3717 = ☐

```
  5749
– 3717
_____
```

8 6468 – 4745 = ☐

```
  6468
– 4745
_____
```

Count up using Frog for one and use the column method for the other.

9 2001 – 1865 = ☐

10 2678 – 1423 = ☐

THINK Do this as a column subtraction. Then do it using Frog. Write a sentence saying which way was better and why.

804 – 382

I am confident with subtracting 3- and 4-digit numbers using column subtraction and counting up.

62

Complete these subtractions. Choose two to answer using Frog and use column subtraction for the rest.

Use Frog if there are zeros in the larger number.

① 7494 – 4624 = ☐

⑤
```
   7342
 – 3268
 _____
```

②
```
   5006
 – 3997
 _____
```

⑥ 7004 – 4989 = ☐

③ 5963 – 3748 = ☐

⑦
```
   8245
 – 5864
 _____
```

④
```
   8096
 – 6846
 _____
```

⑧ 6113 – 4745 = ☐

 **THINK** Write a subtraction which can be done either as a column subtraction or by using Frog. Demonstrate both methods.

I am confident with subtracting 4-digit numbers using column subtraction and counting up.

Answer these subtractions, using the column method.

1. 7494 – 4865 = ☐

2. 5524 – 957 = ☐

3. 6724 – 748 = ☐

4. 6034 – 1452 = ☐

5. 7332 – 4889 = ☐

6. 9506 – 784 = ☐

7. 5054 – 3859 = ☐

8. 8014 – 4667 = ☐

Solve these word problems.

9. Farrah has £4628 in her bank account.
She decides to spend £2850 on a car.
How much money does she have left?

10. Katie has a bowl that weighs 952 g.
She empties some flour into the bowl
and then weighs the bowl and the
flour together. It weighs 2624 g.
How much flour is in the bowl?

1191 – ABC = CBA

A, B, and C are digits between 1 and 9.
No two letters have the same digit number.
Work out what digits A, B and C could be.

○ I am confident with subtracting 3- and 4-digit
○ numbers using column subtraction and counting up.

Finding change

Find the change for each question.
Draw a number line to help you.

1. You have £20 and you spend £11·73.
How much change do you get?

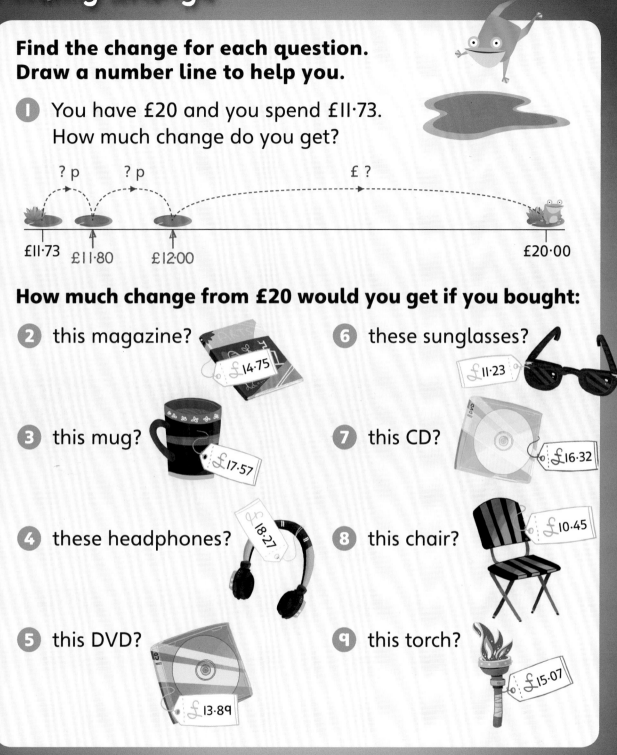

? p   ? p   £ ?

£11·73 £11·80   £12·00   £20·00

How much change from £20 would you get if you bought:

2. this magazine?
£14·75

3. this mug?
£17·57

4. these headphones?
£18·27

5. this DVD?
£13·89

6. these sunglasses?
£11·23

7. this CD?
£16·32

8. this chair?
£10·45

9. this torch?
£15·07

 **THINK** Two toys are the same price and are paid for with £10. If the change is between 20p and 40p, what amounts could the toys cost?

○
○ **I am confident with finding change from £20 using**
○ **the method of counting up.**

Claire has £20. How much change would she get if she bought these items?

1 £12·57

2 £7·75

3 £16·42

4 £17·13

Work out how much money will be left in the wallet after the computer game has been bought.

5 £51·68   £27·88

6 £49·56   £18·78

7 £65·23   £38·45

Solve this problem.

8 Craig has £61·22 in his bank. When a Direct Debit of £19·48 comes out, how much money does Craig have left?

THINK
You have £10. You spend £7·89. Change = ☐
You have £10. You spend £6·78. Change = ☐
You have £10. You spend £5·67. Change = ☐
Continue this pattern.

I am confident with working out change from £20 using the method of counting up.

Solve these problems.

1. Chang has £63·29 in her bank account. She pays a phone bill for £38·64. How much money does Chang have left?

2. An MP4 player costs £77·37. James has saved £67·46. How much more does he need to be able to buy the MP4 player?

3. Chloe has £54·78 in her money box. Chloe's brother has £39·65 in his money box. How much more money does Chloe have than her brother?

4. Jasmine has £92·01 in her bank account. Two payments are made from the account. On Monday a bill for £57·22 is paid and on Tuesday Jasmine pays her £27·49 mobile phone bill. How much money is left in the account?

5. Ben was given £80 for his birthday. He bought a bike helmet for £42·79 and a pair of cycling gloves for £18·45. How much money does he have left?

6. George has £52·72. He buys two DVDs each costing £17·49. How much does he have left and does he have enough to buy a third DVD?

THINK   Three toys are all the same price and are paid for with £10. If the change is less than 50p and more than 10p, what amounts could the toys cost?

I am confident with working out change using the method of counting up.

Coordinates

Write the coordinates of the vertices of each shape.

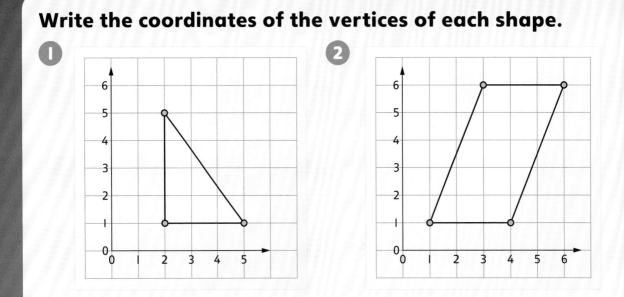

Draw 8 × 8 coordinate grids on squared paper.
Plot the points and join them to make a shape.
Write the name of the shape.

3️⃣ (3, 5), (7, 5), (5, 2)

4️⃣ (2, 3), (2, 6), (6, 3), (6, 6)

5️⃣ (0, 2), (0, 8), (2, 4), (6, 4)

6️⃣ (1, 1), (5, 1), (1, 7), (5, 7), (8, 4)

Plot these points and write a description of each shape.

7️⃣ (1, 0), (3, 2), (4, 7), (5, 2), (7, 0)

8️⃣ (5, 1), (7, 3), (6, 4), (3, 6), (1, 3), (2, 3), (2, 2), (3, 1)

 **THINK** Write coordinates of a square with a missing point. Your partner says the missing coordinate. Repeat for a rectangle.

⬤ **I am confident with reading and plotting**
○ **coordinates to draw polygons.**

Answer these questions.

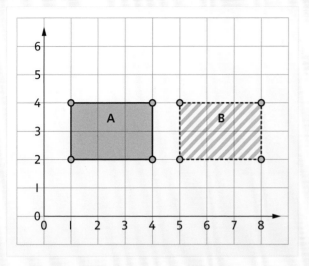

1 Write the coordinates of rectangle A.

2 The rectangle moves four squares to the right, to position B. Write the new coordinates.

3 Rectangle B moves one square up. Write the new coordinates.

4 Write the coordinates of the triangle, C.

5 The triangle moves one square to the left. Write the new coordinates.

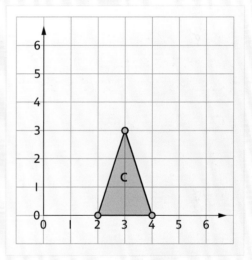

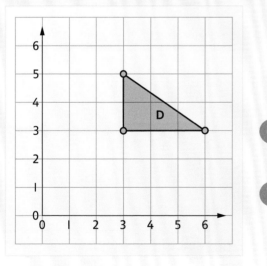

6 Write the coordinates of triangle D.

7 The triangle moves two squares down. Write the new coordinates.

 Two coordinates of a square are (1, 3) and (1, 6). What might be the coordinates of the other two vertices?

I am confident with the translation of shapes using coordinates.

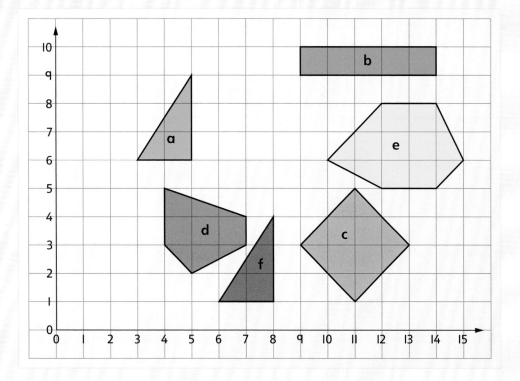

1. Shape a moves three squares to the right.
   Write the new coordinates.

2. Shape b moves two squares down.
   Write the new coordinates.

3. Shape c moves nine squares to the left.
   Write the new coordinates.

4. Shape d moves four squares to the left and
   two squares down. Write the new coordinates.

5. Shape e moves three squares to the left and
   one square up. Write the new coordinates.

 Find a route to slide triangle a to the position
of triangle f. It can only move left, right, up
and down. Then describe a different route.

I am confident with using coordinates to
describe position.

Bar charts and pictograms

This bar chart shows the lengths of five films. Answer the questions.

1 Which film is the longest?

2 How many minutes longer is Film 1 than Film 4?

3 Which Film is about 30 minutes shorter than Film 3?

4 What is the total length of Films 1 and 3 altogether?

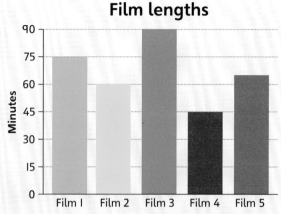

Film lengths

This pictogram shows the number of different types of films that Joe has in his collection.

5 How many Horror films does he have?

6 How many more Children's films does he have than Drama films?

7 Draw a bar chart to show the same information.

Types of films

Comedy	◯ ◯ ◯ ◯
Horror	◯ ◯
Children's	◯ ◯ ◯
Drama	◯

◯ = 2 films

THINK Millie saw 12 shrews, 8 mice, 3 sparrows, 3 blackbirds and 1 weasel in her garden. She draws a bar chart to show this information. How much taller is the shrew's bar than the blackbird's bar? Which two bars are the same heights? How many creatures did she see in total?

⬤ I am confident with reading and drawing bar
◯ charts and pictograms.
◯
◯

Answer the questions about the pictogram. Then draw a bar chart that shows the same information.

Length of songs in the Top 40

2 min	⬤ ⬤	
2 min 15 s	⬤ ⬤	
2 min 30 s	⬤ ⬤ ⬤	
2 min 45 s	⬤ ⬤	
3 min	⬤	

⬤ = 4 songs

1 How many songs in the Top 40 are 2 min 45 s long?

2 There are 12 songs that are the same length. How long are they?

3 Which length of song is the least common?

4 How many more songs are 2 min long than are 3 min long?

5 How many songs are either 2 min 15 s or 2 min 30 s long?

6 How many songs are less than 3 min long?

THINK Oliver watched a bird table for an hour. 32 birds visited it. Of these, 15 were blue tits and 2 were robins. The rest were equal numbers of siskins, green finches and starlings. In Oliver's pictogram, 1 square represents 2 birds. How many squares will he need to draw for the starlings?

○ I am confident with using pictograms to draw
○ bar charts.
○

Line graphs

Look at the line graph and answer the questions.

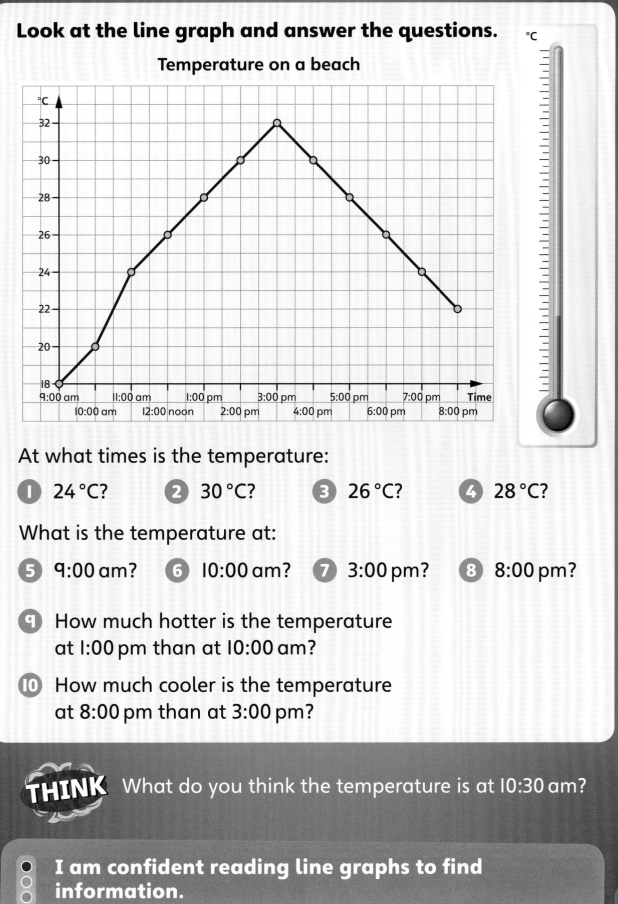

Temperature on a beach

At what times is the temperature:

1. 24 °C?   2. 30 °C?   3. 26 °C?   4. 28 °C?

What is the temperature at:

5. 9:00 am?   6. 10:00 am?   7. 3:00 pm?   8. 8:00 pm?

9. How much hotter is the temperature at 1:00 pm than at 10:00 am?

10. How much cooler is the temperature at 8:00 pm than at 3:00 pm?

THINK What do you think the temperature is at 10:30 am?

I am confident reading line graphs to find information.

Look at the line graph and answer the questions.

Temperature in a classroom

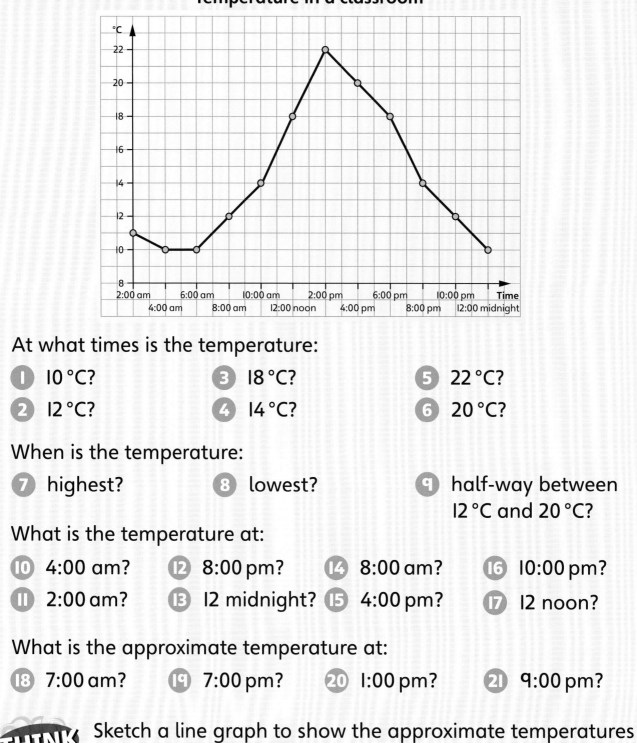

At what times is the temperature:

1 10 °C?

2 12 °C?

3 18 °C?

4 14 °C?

5 22 °C?

6 20 °C?

When is the temperature:

7 highest?

8 lowest?

9 half-way between 12 °C and 20 °C?

What is the temperature at:

10 4:00 am?

11 2:00 am?

12 8:00 pm?

13 12 midnight?

14 8:00 am?

15 4:00 pm?

16 10:00 pm?

17 12 noon?

What is the approximate temperature at:

18 7:00 am?

19 7:00 pm?

20 1:00 pm?

21 9:00 pm?

THINK Sketch a line graph to show the approximate temperatures in your classroom over the school day. Show how the temperatures might change throughout the day.

 **I am confident with using line graphs to find information.**

74

Look at the information below. Draw a line graph to show the temperatures over the course of the day.

Time	8:00 am	10:00 am	12:00 pm	2:00 pm
Temperature in °C	8	12	14	16

Time	4:00 pm	6:00 pm	8:00 pm	10:00 pm
Temperature in °C	18	16	10	6

Now answer the questions using your line graph.

At what times is the temperature:

1 16 °C? 2 10 °C? 3 8 °C? 4 13 °C?

What is the approximate temperature at:

5 9:00 am? 6 1:00 pm? 7 3:00 pm? 8 5:00 pm?

9 How much hotter is the temperature at 6:00 pm than at 10:00 am?

10 How much cooler is the temperature at 10:00 pm than at 10:00 am?

11 Estimate the approximate time in the evening when the temperature is 7 °C.

12 Do you think that the temperature might have got above 18 °C during this day? Explain your answer.

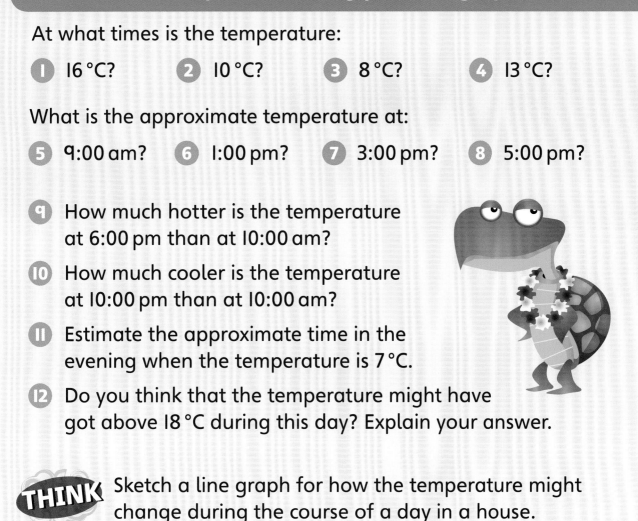

THINK Sketch a line graph for how the temperature might change during the course of a day in a house.

● I am confident with drawing line graphs using
○ given information.
○

Multiplying 3-digit numbers by 1-digit numbers

Work out how far the aeroplane can fly.

A Boeing 747 aircraft flies at a speed of 567 mph.

1 How far can the aircraft fly in 2 hours?

> mph stands for 'miles per hour'.

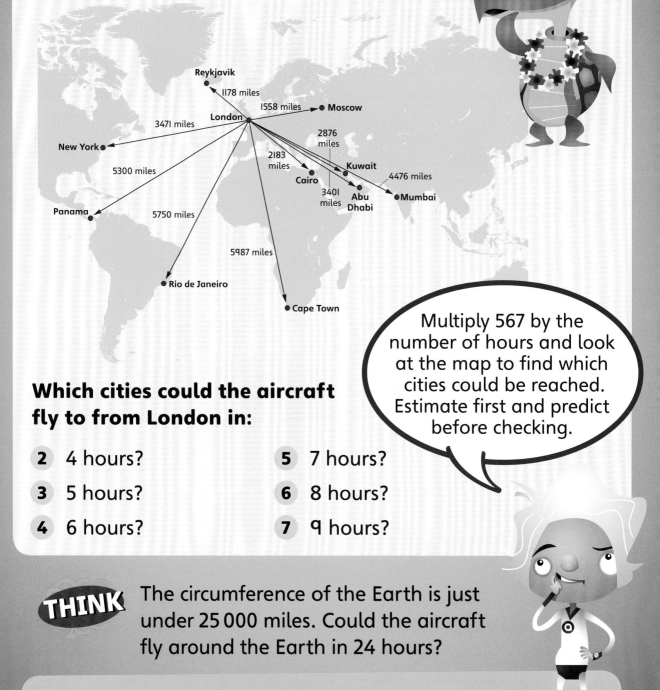

Which cities could the aircraft fly to from London in:

2 4 hours?

3 5 hours?

4 6 hours?

5 7 hours?

6 8 hours?

7 9 hours?

> Multiply 567 by the number of hours and look at the map to find which cities could be reached. Estimate first and predict before checking.

THINK The circumference of the Earth is just under 25 000 miles. Could the aircraft fly around the Earth in 24 hours?

● I am confident with multiplying 3-digit
○ numbers by 1-digit numbers.

76

Work out the cost of the air tickets.

1 An air ticket to India costs £468.
   5 people want to go together.
   What is the total cost of their tickets?

2 An air ticket to Australia costs £829. 3 people want
   to go together. What is the total cost of their tickets?

3 4 people want to travel to India and 6 people want to
   travel to Australia. What is the total cost of their tickets?

4 Which is cheaper and by how much: 6 tickets
   to India or 4 tickets to Australia?

5 James wants to buy 5 tickets to Australia. He has saved
   £4000. How much more money does he need?

Use estimation to work out the missing numbers. Then use multiplication to check your answers.

6 $345 \times \boxed{} = 1725$

7 $\boxed{} \times 187 = 1122$

8 $294 \times \boxed{} = 1176$

9 $\boxed{} \times 621 = 4347$

10 $\boxed{} \times 717 = 3585$

11 $867 \times \boxed{} = 5202$

12 $\boxed{} \times 649 = 5841$

13 $468 \times \boxed{} = 3276$

 What multiple of 25 can be
multiplied by 9 to give 2025?

- I am confident with multiplying 3-digit numbers
  by 1-digit numbers.

Use a written method to work out the answer to each question.

$7 \times 346 = \square$

×	300	40	6
7	2100	280	42

$$\begin{array}{r} 346 \\ \times \quad 7 \\ \hline 2100 \\ 280 \\ + \quad 42 \\ \hline 2422 \end{array}$$

2100 ← 7 × 300
280 ← 7 × 40
42 ← 7 × 6

THINK Which of your answers do you think will be more than 3000? Which answers do you think will be less than 3000?

1 $6 \times 263 = \square$

2 $4 \times 425 = \square$

3 $7 \times 336 = \square$

4 $743 \times 8 = \square$

5 $9 \times 346 = \square$

6 $716 \times 4 = \square$

7 $292 \times 8 = \square$

8 $9 \times 178 = \square$

9 $664 \times 7 = \square$

10 $5 \times 793 = \square$

● I am confident with multiplying 3-digit numbers
○ by 1-digit numbers.

Adding fractions

Add these fractions. Use the pizza slices to help you.

1. $\dfrac{2}{6} + \dfrac{2}{6} = \dfrac{\square}{\square}$

3. $\dfrac{1}{6} + \dfrac{5}{6} = \dfrac{\square}{\square}$

2. $\dfrac{3}{6} + \dfrac{2}{6} = \dfrac{\square}{\square}$

4. $\dfrac{3}{6} + \dfrac{3}{6} = \dfrac{\square}{\square}$

Add these fractions. Use the pizza slices to help you.

5. $\dfrac{1}{8} + \dfrac{4}{8} = \dfrac{\square}{\square}$

7. $\dfrac{5}{8} + \dfrac{3}{8} = \dfrac{\square}{\square}$

6. $\dfrac{3}{8} + \dfrac{4}{8} = \dfrac{\square}{\square}$

8. $\dfrac{6}{8} + \dfrac{1}{8} = \dfrac{\square}{\square}$

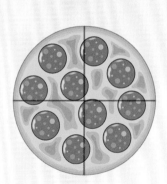

Add these fractions. Use the pizza slices to help you.

9. $\dfrac{1}{4} + \dfrac{3}{4} = \dfrac{\square}{\square}$

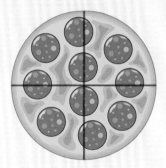
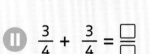

10. $\dfrac{3}{4} + \dfrac{2}{4} = \dfrac{\square}{\square}$

11. $\dfrac{3}{4} + \dfrac{3}{4} = \dfrac{\square}{\square}$

THINK Write two fraction additions not on the page, one with an answer greater than 1 and one with an answer less than 1.

○ **I am confident with adding fractions.**
○
○

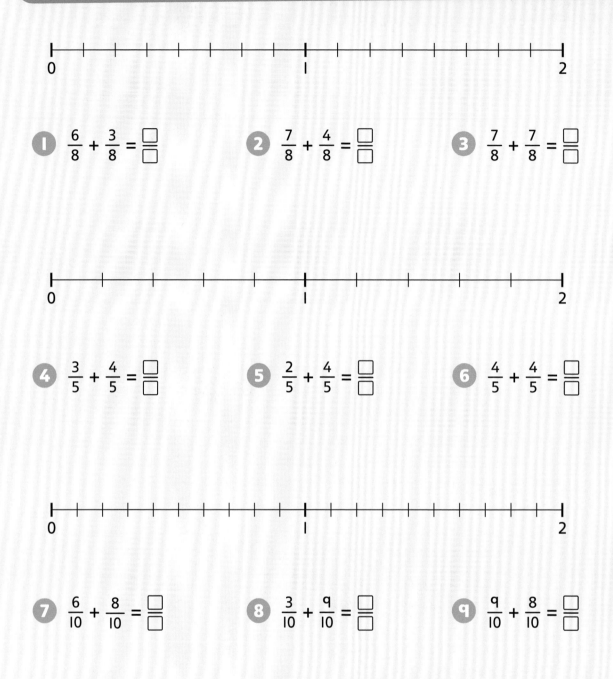

1 $\frac{6}{8} + \frac{3}{8} = \frac{\Box}{\Box}$

2 $\frac{7}{8} + \frac{4}{8} = \frac{\Box}{\Box}$

3 $\frac{7}{8} + \frac{7}{8} = \frac{\Box}{\Box}$

4 $\frac{3}{5} + \frac{4}{5} = \frac{\Box}{\Box}$

5 $\frac{2}{5} + \frac{4}{5} = \frac{\Box}{\Box}$

6 $\frac{4}{5} + \frac{4}{5} = \frac{\Box}{\Box}$

7 $\frac{6}{10} + \frac{8}{10} = \frac{\Box}{\Box}$

8 $\frac{3}{10} + \frac{9}{10} = \frac{\Box}{\Box}$

9 $\frac{9}{10} + \frac{8}{10} = \frac{\Box}{\Box}$

 Write two fraction additions not on the page with answers less than 1. Then write two more additions with answers more than 1.

I am confident with adding fractions.

Write the number that will come out of each machine.

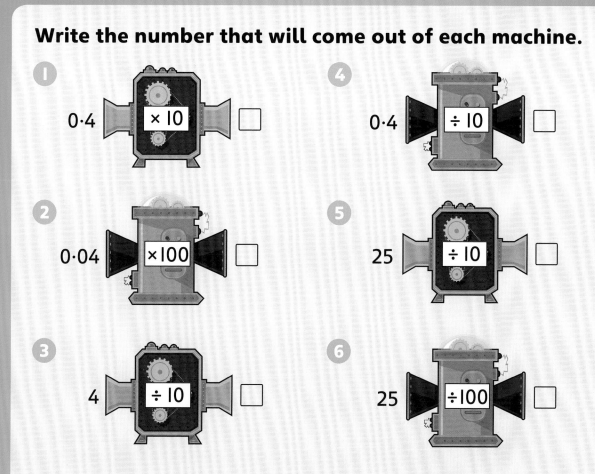

1. 0.4 ×10 ☐

2. 0.04 ×100 ☐

3. 4 ÷10 ☐

4. 0.4 ÷10 ☐

5. 25 ÷10 ☐

6. 25 ÷100 ☐

Write the outputs for this 2-step function machine.
What single function machine could replace it?

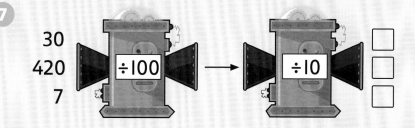

7. 30
   420
   7
   ÷100 → ÷10 ☐ ☐ ☐

THINK Design a 3-step function machine where the numbers that come out of the third machine are the same as the numbers that went into the first machine.

○ **I am confident with multiplying and dividing by 10 and 100.**

Write the missing outputs or inputs for these function machines.

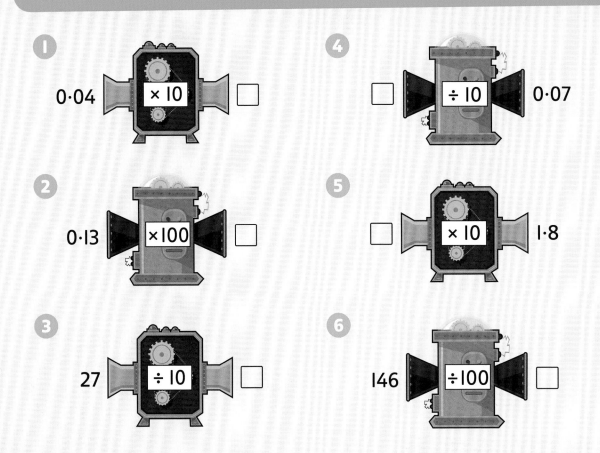

① 0·04 [× 10] ☐

④ ☐ [÷ 10] 0·07

② 0·13 [×100] ☐

⑤ ☐ [× 10] 1·8

③ 27 [÷ 10] ☐

⑥ 146 [÷100] ☐

Write the missing inputs and outputs for this 2-step function machine. What single function machine could replace it?

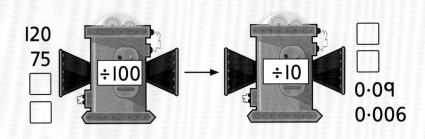

⑦
120
75
☐
☐
[÷100] → [÷10]
☐
☐
0·09
0·006

THINK If $\frac{1}{2}$ goes into a function machine that multiplies by 10, what number will come out? If $1\frac{1}{2}$ goes in, what will come out?

● **I am confident with multiplying and dividing by**
○ **10 and 100.**
○

Multiplying by 11 and 12

Football teams have 11 players. Work out how many players there are in each county.

1. Devon: 35 teams

2. Oxfordshire: 46 teams

3. Yorkshire: 38 teams

4. Nottinghamshire: 19 teams

5. Cumbria: 27 teams

6. Greater London: 53 teams

Eggs come in boxes of a dozen. Calculate how many eggs each restaurant orders.

7. Hannah and Harry's Bistro: 37 boxes

8. Jimmy's Diner: 43 boxes

9. Claire's Café: 29 boxes

10. Ben's Breakfast Bar: 54 boxes

11. The Spaghetti House: 26 boxes

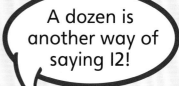

A dozen is another way of saying 12!

 THINK Work out 11 × 63. What would be a quick way of working out 12 × 63?

● I am confident with multiplying 2-digit numbers
● by 11 and 12.

Multiplying two 2-digit numbers

Copy and complete the multiplication grids.

1 12 × 32

×	30	2	
10	300	20	= 320
2	60	4	= 64

4 12 × 28

×	20	8	
10			=
2			=

2 12 × 43

×	40	3	
10			=
2			=

5 12 × 34

×	30	4	
10			=
2			=

3 12 × 26

×	20	6	
10			=
2			=

6 12 × 48

×	40	8	
10			=
2			=

 **THINK** Choose a 2-digit number. Multiply it by 6. Now multiply it by 12. What do you notice? Why do you think this is?

● I am confident with multiplying 2-digit numbers by 12 using the grid method.

Copy and complete the multiplication grids.

1 15 × 32

×	30	2	
10	300	20	=
5	150	10	= ___

3 13 × 36

×	30	6	
10			=
3			= ___

2 14 × 43

×	40	3	
10			=
4			= ___

4 16 × 24

×	20	4	
10			=
6			= ___

Work these multiplications out using the same method.

5 13 × 21 = ☐

6 14 × 28 = ☐

7 16 × 24 = ☐

8 15 × 25 = ☐

9 14 × 27 = ☐

10 13 × 29 = ☐

 **THINK** Do you think 13 × 25 will give the same answer as 15 × 23? Make a prediction and then test it.

⦁
⦁ **I am confident with multiplying 2-digit numbers**
⦁ **by teen numbers.**

Complete these multiplications.

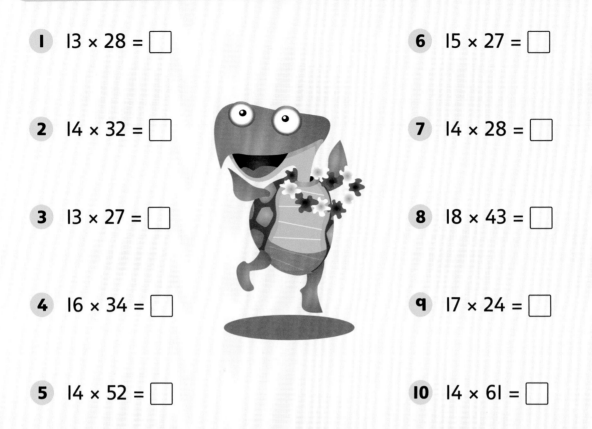

1 13 × 28 = ☐

2 14 × 32 = ☐

3 13 × 27 = ☐

4 16 × 34 = ☐

5 14 × 52 = ☐

6 15 × 27 = ☐

7 14 × 28 = ☐

8 18 × 43 = ☐

9 17 × 24 = ☐

10 14 × 61 = ☐

Solve these word problems.

11 The school cook has ordered 32 trays of a dozen eggs. How many eggs has she ordered?

12 Mrs Hatfield has sent 47 texts at 13p each this month. How much will she be charged for texts this month?

THINK Which two teen numbers multiply to give an answer of 221?

• I am confident with multiplying 2-digit numbers
○ by teen numbers.

Complete these multiplications.

25 × 34

×	30	4	
20	600	80	= 680
5	150	20	= 170

$$\begin{array}{r} 680 \\ 170 \\ \hline 850 \end{array}$$

1   24 × 45

×	40	5	
20			=
4			=

_____

2   26 × 42 = ☐

3   27 × 51 = ☐

4   32 × 46 = ☐

5   35 × 48 = ☐

6   28 × 36 = ☐

7   25 × 53 = ☐

THINK What multiple of 5 is multiplied by 41 to give a product of 1025?

● I am confident with multiplying two 2-digit
○ numbers using the grid method.
○

Answer these multiplications using the grid method.

 THINK Which of these multiplications will have the smallest answer? Which will have the largest answer?

1 27 × 37 = ☐

2 28 × 53 = ☐

3 36 × 45 = ☐

4 25 × 57 = ☐

5 37 × 47 = ☐

6 34 × 56 = ☐

7 32 × 57 = ☐

8 23 × 58 = ☐

Solve these word problems.

9 A school has 23 classes of children with 32 children in each class. How many children are there altogether in the school?

10 A stamp costs 36p and you are sending 45 greetings cards. How much will you have to pay for them all?

11 Jane gives out 26 goodie bags, one to each member of her class, to celebrate her birthday. If each bag costs 58p, how much was spent on the goodie bags?

● I am confident with multiplying pairs of 2-digit
○ numbers using the grid method.

Finding fractions of amounts

These families are travelling by train. Each person pays the same amount. How much does one ticket cost?

① Manchester £46

④ Leeds £28

⑦ York £66

② Hull £63

⑤ Lincoln £39

⑧ Grimsby £48

③ Nottingham £55

⑥ Leicester £70

⑨ Newcastle £25

THINK The trip to Bournemouth is £72. Write the cost for 2 people, 3 people and 4 people.

Complete these calculations.

⑩ $\frac{1}{3}$ of 21 kg, $\frac{2}{3}$ of 21 kg

⑪ $\frac{1}{5}$ of 45 kg, $\frac{3}{5}$ of 45 kg

⑫ $\frac{1}{4}$ of 36 kg, $\frac{3}{4}$ of 36 kg

⑬ $\frac{1}{6}$ of 42 kg, $\frac{5}{6}$ of 42 kg

⑭ $\frac{1}{8}$ of 48 kg, $\frac{5}{8}$ of 48 kg

⑮ $\frac{1}{10}$ of 60 kg, $\frac{3}{10}$ of 60 kg

I am confident with finding fractions of 2-digit amounts.

Write how much each child has saved.

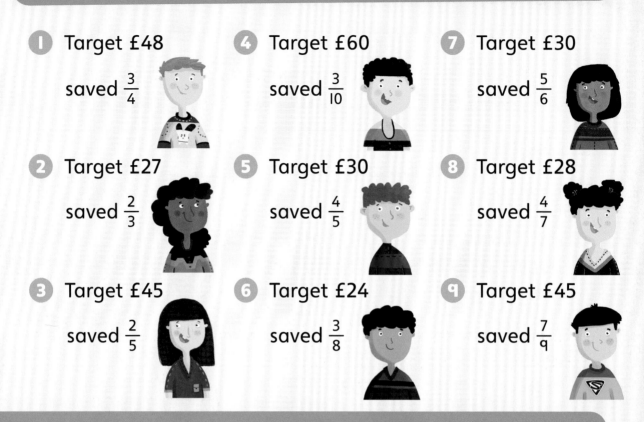

1. Target £48 saved $\frac{3}{4}$

2. Target £27 saved $\frac{2}{3}$

3. Target £45 saved $\frac{2}{5}$

4. Target £60 saved $\frac{3}{10}$

5. Target £30 saved $\frac{4}{5}$

6. Target £24 saved $\frac{3}{8}$

7. Target £30 saved $\frac{5}{6}$

8. Target £28 saved $\frac{4}{7}$

9. Target £45 saved $\frac{7}{9}$

Find the fractions of each amount.

10. $\frac{7}{10}$ of 80 g = ☐

11. $\frac{3}{4}$ of 12 km = ☐

12. $\frac{5}{6}$ of 300 ml = ☐

13. $\frac{7}{9}$ of 18 m = ☐

14. $\frac{3}{8}$ of 40 l = ☐

15. $\frac{2}{7}$ of 63 kg = ☐

16. $\frac{4}{6}$ of 18 g = ☐

17. $\frac{2}{3}$ of 24 cm = ☐

18. $\frac{5}{7}$ of 63 l = ☐

 **THINK** You need £60 more to reach a target. What fraction could you have saved, and what could your target be? For example, you could have saved $\frac{1}{2}$ of a target of £120.

● ○ ○ ○ **I am confident with finding fractions of 2- and 3-digit amounts.**

Solving problems

Solve these problems.

1. At an ice rink, there are 148 people on the ice. 67 more people go on to the ice. How many are there now?

2. Skate hire costs £4. If 183 people hired skates, how much did they pay in total?

3. Urvi goes to the ice rink 18 times each month. How many times does she go to the ice rink each year (12 months)?

4. Dinesh spends £4·78 on snacks at the café. How much change will he get from £10·00?

5. On Monday £716 was spent on hiring skates. How many people paid £4 each for skate hire?

6. It costs £4·85 for a child and £6·40 for an adult to go into the ice rink. How much does it cost for two children and an adult?

7. Mr Jones buys a £6·40 ticket and two £4·85 tickets. He also pays for three pairs of skates at £4 per pair. How much change will he get from £30?

 THINK Make up your own ice rink word problem.

○ **I am confident with choosing a method to solve**
○ **problems using all four operations.**

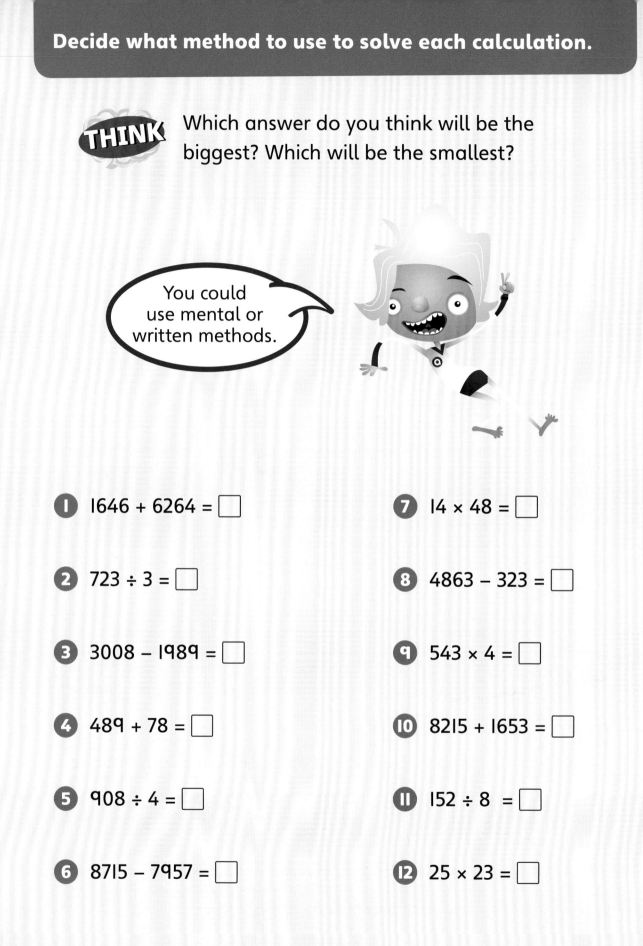

THINK Which answer do you think will be the biggest? Which will be the smallest?

You could use mental or written methods.

1. $1646 + 6264 = \square$

2. $723 \div 3 = \square$

3. $3008 - 1989 = \square$

4. $489 + 78 = \square$

5. $908 \div 4 = \square$

6. $8715 - 7957 = \square$

7. $14 \times 48 = \square$

8. $4863 - 323 = \square$

9. $543 \times 4 = \square$

10. $8215 + 1653 = \square$

11. $152 \div 8 = \square$

12. $25 \times 23 = \square$

Practising calculations

1 5099 + 100 = ☐
5099 − 100 = ☐
5099 + 1000 = ☐
5099 − 1000 = ☐

2 13·7 + ☐ = 14

3 121 ÷ 11 = ☐

4 £77·22 + £13·61 = ☐

5 3008 − 1989 = ☐

6 4 × 827 = ☐

7 3 × 406 = ☐

8
8096
− 6846
‾‾‾‾‾

9 45 + 48 = ☐
745 + 48 = ☐
7445 + 48 = ☐

10 ☐ × 12 = 84

11 £48·52 + £37·57 = ☐

12 14 × 61 = ☐

13 14 × 52 = ☐

14 8 × 202 = ☐

15 8215 + 1653 = ☐

16 5 × 734 = ☐

17
6113
− 4745
‾‾‾‾‾

18 On Monday £724 was spent on hiring skates. How many people paid £4 each for skate hire?

19 Craig has £61·22 in his bank. When a Direct Debit of £17·88 comes out, how much money does Craig have left?

20 In July a sunflower is $1\frac{1}{2}$ m tall. By August it has grown 60 cm taller. How tall is it in August?

21 A hedge is 2·81 m tall. Izzy cuts $\frac{1}{2}$ m from the top of the hedge. How tall is the hedge now?

Grid investigations

Work with a partner.

1 Estimate how many numbers are in this grid.
Then count to check.

9·2	9·65	9·7	30·9	8·4	7·51	70	3·62	60	8·1
33·3	3	10·2	10·9	15·6	7·99	34	11·8	5·9	10·7
8·94	30·1	19·0	11·1	11·8	20	8·79	11·3	4·44	45·6
18·5	77·3	909	35	12	4·6	6	26·5	8·8	1·29
5·5	2·52	2·65	545	12·3	6·09	7·34	100	8	13·9
2·25	5·3	50	13·2	13	87·8	90	6·4	1·54	5·86
32	22·2	14	13·5	99·9	31·1	9·19	4·3	1·25	46
7·77	3·91	14·6	4·8	1·39	7·42	21·4	289	95	1·7

2 Find a number in the grid that lies between:
a) 8 and 9   c) 11 and 12
b) 30 and 31   d) 7·5 and 7·6

3 Write the yellow numbers in order from smallest to largest.

4 **Follow a trail.** Start at 9.7 . Move down or across (not diagonally). The numbers must get bigger each time. Which number do you finish on?

5 Choose 3 blue numbers and split them into 1s, tenths and hundredths like this: 2·65 = 2 + 0·6 + 0·05

6 Write the green numbers in order, largest to smallest.

7 How many [blue numbers] have 9 as their tenths digit? Which numbers are they?

8 About how many [pink numbers] are there? Explain how you estimated the answer.

9 Round each [yellow number] to the nearest 10. Which is the odd one out?

10 If I round the [yellow numbers] to the nearest whole number, two numbers have the answer, 6. Which numbers are they?

11 Choose three [blue numbers] and round them to the nearest whole number.

Can you solve these puzzles by finding matching numbers from the multicoloured grid?

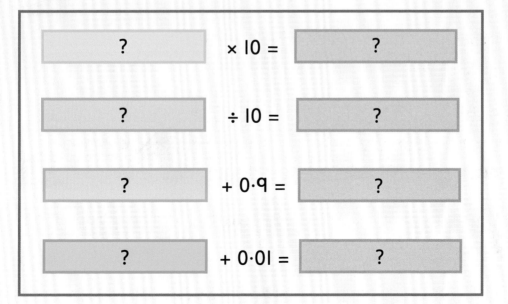

[?] × 10 = [?]

[?] ÷ 10 = [?]

[?] + 0·9 = [?]

[?] + 0·01 = [?]

Series Editor
Ruth Merttens

Author Team
Jennie Kerwin and Hilda Merttens

Published by Pearson Education Limited, Edinburgh Gate, Harlow, Essex, CM20 2JE.

www.pearsonschools.co.uk

Text © Pearson Education Limited 2014
Page design and layout by room9design
Original illustrations © Pearson Education Limited 2014
Illustrated by Villie Karabatzia pp12, 21–22, 27–28, 40, 42, 45–47, 50–51, 60–61, 64–67, 71–72, 77, 83, 86, 88–91, 93;
Matt Buckley pp10–11, 15–17, 31–36, 38–39, 49, 52–54, 68–74, 76, 79–80; Andrew Painter pp81–82; Bill Ledger pp41
Cover design by Pearson Education Limited
Cover illustration and Abacus character artwork by Volker Beisler © Pearson Education Limited
Additional contributions by Hilary Koll and Steve Mills, CME Projects Ltd.

First published 2014

16 15 14
10 9 8 7 6 5 4 3 2

British Library Cataloguing in Publication Data
A catalogue record for this book is available from the British Library

ISBN 978 1 408 27852 9

Printed in Slovakia

Acknowledgements
We would like to thank the staff and pupils at North Kidlington Primary School, Haydon Wick Primary School, Swindon, St Mary's Catholic Primary School, Bodmin, St Andrew's C of E Primary & Nursery School, Sutton-in-Ashfield, Saint James' C of E Primary School, Southampton and Harborne Primary School, Birmingham, for their invaluable help in the development and trialling of this book.

Every effort has been made to contact copyright holders of material reproduced in this book. Any omissions will be rectified in subsequent printings if notice is given to the publishers.